Martin Luther King, Jr.

A Tough Mind and a Tender Heart

D1332236

PENGUIN BOOKS — GREAT IDEAS

PENGUIN BOOKS

UK | USA | Canada | Ireland | Australia
India | New Zealand | South Africa

Penguin Books is part of the Penguin Random House group
of companies whose addresses can be found at
global.penguinrandomhouse.com.

First published in *Why We Can't Wait*, 1963 and
A Gift of Love, 2012, by Beacon Press
This selection first published in Penguin Books 2020
001

Copyright © Martin Luther King, Jr., 1963, 1964
Copyright renewed © Coretta Scott King, Dexter King, Martin
Luther King III, Yolanda King, Bernice King, 1986

Set in 11.2/13.75 pt Dante MT Std
Typeset by Jouve (UK), Milton Keynes
Printed and bound in Great Britain by Clays Ltd, Elcograf S.p.A.

A CIP catalogue record for this book
is available from the British Library

ISBN: 978–0–241–47325–2

www.greenpenguin.co.uk

MIX
Paper from
responsible sources
FSC® C018179

Penguin Random House is committed to a
sustainable future for our business, our readers
and our planet. This book is made from Forest
Stewardship Council® certified paper.

Contents

A Tough Mind and a Tender Heart

Be ye therefore wise as serpents, and harmless as doves.
MATTHEW 10:16

A French philosopher said, 'No man is strong unless he bears within his character antitheses strongly marked.' The strong man holds in a living blend strongly marked opposites. Not ordinarily do men achieve this balance of opposites. The idealists are not usually realistic, and the realists are not usually idealistic. The militant are not generally known to be passive, nor the passive to be militant. Seldom are the humble self-assertive, or the self-assertive humble. But life at its best is a creative synthesis of opposites in fruitful harmony. The philosopher Hegel said that truth is found neither in the thesis nor the antithesis, but in an emergent synthesis which reconciles the two.

Jesus recognized the need for blending opposites. He knew that his disciples would face a difficult and hostile world, where they would confront the recalcitrance of political officials and the intransigence of the protectors of the old order. He knew that they would meet cold and arrogant men whose hearts had been hardened by the long winter of traditionalism. So he said to them,

'Behold, I send you forth as sheep in the midst of wolves.' And he gave them a formula for action, 'Be ye therefore wise as serpents, and harmless as doves.' It is pretty difficult to imagine a single person having, simultaneously, the characteristics of the serpent and the dove, but this is what Jesus expects. We must combine the toughness of the serpent and the softness of the dove, a tough mind and a tender heart.

I

Let us consider, first, the need for a tough mind, characterized by incisive thinking, realistic appraisal, and decisive judgment. The tough mind is sharp and penetrating, breaking through the crust of legends and myths and sifting the true from the false. The tough minded individual is astute and discerning. He has a strong, austere quality that makes for firmness of purpose and solidness of commitment.

Who doubts that this toughness of mind is one of man's greatest needs? Rarely do we find men who willingly engage in hard, solid thinking. There is an almost universal quest for easy answers and half-baked solutions. Nothing pains some people more than having to think.

This prevalent tendency toward softmindedness is found in man's unbelievable gullibility. Take our attitude toward advertisements. We are so easily led to purchase a product because a television or radio advertisement pronounces it better than any other.

Advertisers have long since learned that most people are softminded, and they capitalize on this susceptibility with skillful and effective slogans.

This undue gullibility is also seen in the tendency of many readers to accept the printed word of the press as final truth. Few people realize that even our authentic channels of information – the press, the platform, and in many instances the pulpit – do not give us objective and unbiased truth. Few people have the toughness of mind to judge critically and to discern the true from the false, the fact from the fiction. Our minds are constantly being invaded by legions of half-truths, prejudices, and false facts. One of the great needs of man-kind is to be lifted above the morass of false propaganda.

Softminded individuals are prone to embrace all kinds of superstitions. Their minds are constantly invaded by irrational fears, which range from fear of Friday the thirteenth to fear of a black cat crossing one's path. As the elevator made its upward climb in one of the large hotels of New York City, I noticed for the first time that there was no thirteenth floor – floor fourteen followed floor twelve. On inquiring from the elevator operator the reason for this omission, he said, 'This practice is followed by most large hotels because of the fear of numerous people to stay on a thirteenth floor.' Then he added, 'The real foolishness of the fear is to be found in the fact that the fourteenth floor is actually the thirteenth.' Such fears leave the soft mind haggard by day and haunted by night.

The softminded man always fears change. He feels

security in the status quo, and he has an almost morbid fear of the new. For him, the greatest pain is the pain of a new idea. An elderly segregationist in the South is reported to have said, 'I have come to see now that desegregation is inevitable. But I pray God that it will not take place until after I die.' The softminded person always wants to freeze the moment and hold life in the gripping yoke of sameness.

Softmindedness often invades religion. This is why religion has sometimes rejected new truth with a dogmatic passion. Through edicts and bulls, inquisitions and excommunications, the church has attempted to prorogue truth and place an impenetrable stone wall in the path of the truth-seeker. The historical-philological criticism of the Bible is considered by the softminded as blasphemous, and reason is often looked upon as the exercise of a corrupt faculty. Softminded persons have revised the Beatitudes to read, 'Blessed are the pure in ignorance: for they shall see God.'

This has also led to a widespread belief that there is a conflict between science and religion. But this is not true. There may be a conflict between softminded religionists and toughminded scientists, but not between science and religion. Their respective worlds are different and their methods are dissimilar. Science investigates; religion interprets. Science gives man knowledge which is power; religion gives man wisdom which is control. Science deals mainly with facts; religion deals mainly with values. The two are not rivals. They are complementary. Science keeps religion from sinking into the valley of crippling irrationalism and paralyzing obscurantism. Religion prevents science from falling into the marsh of obsolete materialism and moral nihilism.

We do not need to look far to detect the dangers of softmindedness. Dictators, capitalizing on softmindedness, have led men to acts of barbarity and terror that are unthinkable in civilized society. Adolf Hitler realized that softmindedness was so prevalent among his followers that he said, 'I use emotion for the many and reserve reason for the few.' In *Mein Kampf* he asserted:

> By means of shrewd lies, unremittingly repeated,
> it is possible to make people believe that heaven
> is hell – and hell, heaven . . . The greater the lie,
> the more readily will it be believed.

Softmindedness is one of the basic causes of race prejudice. The toughminded person always examines the facts before he reaches conclusions; in short, he postjudges. The tenderminded person reaches a conclusion before he has examined the first fact; in short, he prejudges and is prejudiced. Race prejudice is based on groundless fears, suspicions, and misunderstandings. There are those who are sufficiently softminded to believe in the superiority of the white race and the inferiority of the Negro race in spite of the toughminded research of anthropologists who reveal the falsity of such a notion. There are softminded persons who argue that racial segregation should be perpetuated because Negroes lag behind in academic, health, and moral standards. They are not toughminded enough to realize that lagging standards are the result of segregation and discrimination. They do not recognize that it is rationally unsound and sociologically untenable to use the tragic effects of segregation as an argument for its continuation. Too many politicians in the South recognize this disease of softmindedness which engulfs their constituency. With insidious zeal, they make inflammatory statements and disseminate distortions and half-truths which arouse abnormal fears and morbid antipathies within the minds of uneducated and underprivileged whites, leaving them so confused that they are led to acts of meanness and violence which no normal person commits.

There is little hope for us until we become toughminded enough to break loose from the shackles of prejudice, half-truths, and downright ignorance. The shape of the world today does not permit us the luxury of softmindedness. A nation or a civilization that continues to produce softminded men purchases its own spiritual death on an installment plan.

II

But we must not stop with the cultivation of a tough mind. The gospel also demands a tender heart. Toughmindedness without tenderheartedness is cold and detached, leaving one's life in a perpetual winter devoid of the warmth of spring and the gentle heat of summer. What is more tragic than to see a person who has risen to the disciplined heights of toughmindedness but has at the same time sunk to the passionless depths of hardheartedness?

The hardhearted person never truly loves. He engages in a crass utilitarianism which values other people mainly according to their usefulness to him. He never experiences the beauty of friendship, because he is too cold to feel affection for another and is too self-centered to share another's joy and sorrow. He is an isolated island. No outpouring of love links him with the mainland of humanity.

The hardhearted person lacks the capacity for genuine compassion. He is unmoved by the pains and afflictions of his brothers. He passes unfortunate men every day, but he never really sees them. He gives dollars to a worthwhile charity, but he gives not of his spirit.

The hardhearted individual never sees people as people, but rather as mere objects or as impersonal cogs in an ever-turning wheel. In the vast wheel of industry, he sees men as hands. In the massive wheel of big city life, he sees men as digits in a multitude. In the deadly wheel of army life, he sees men as numbers in a regiment. He depersonalizes life.

Jesus frequently illustrated the characteristics of the hardhearted. The rich fool was condemned, not because he was not toughminded, but rather because he was not tenderhearted. Life for him was a mirror in which he saw only himself, and not a window through which he saw other selves. Dives went to hell, not because he was wealthy, but because he was not tenderhearted enough to see Lazarus and because he made no attempt to bridge the gulf between himself and his brother.

Jesus reminds us that the good life combines the toughness of the serpent and the tenderness of the dove. To have serpentlike qualities devoid of dovelike qualities is to be passionless, mean, and selfish. To have dovelike without serpentlike qualities is to be sentimental, anemic, and aimless. We must combine strongly marked antitheses.

We as Negroes must bring together toughmindedness and tenderheartedness if we are to move creatively toward the goal of freedom and justice. Softminded individuals among us feel that the only way to deal with oppression is by adjusting to it. They acquiesce and resign themselves to segregation. They prefer to remain oppressed. When Moses led the children of Israel from the slavery of Egypt to the freedom of the Promised Land, he discovered that slaves do not always welcome their deliverers. They would rather bear those ills they have, as Shakespeare pointed out, than flee to others that they know not of. They prefer the 'fleshpots of Egypt' to the ordeals of emancipation. But this is not the way out. Softminded acquiescence is cowardly. My friends, we cannot win the respect of the white people of the South or elsewhere if we are willing to trade the future of our children for our personal safety and comfort. Moreover, we must learn that passively to accept an unjust system is to cooperate with that system, and thereby to become a participant in its evil.

And there are hardhearted and bitter individuals

among us who would combat the opponent with physical violence and corroding hatred. Violence brings only temporary victories; violence, by creating many more social problems than it solves, never brings permanent peace. I am convinced that if we succumb to the temptation to use violence in our struggle for freedom, unborn generations will be the recipients of a long and desolate night of bitterness, and our chief legacy to them will be a never-ending reign of chaos. A Voice, echoing through the corridors of time, says to every intemperate Peter, 'Put up thy sword.' History is cluttered with the wreckage of nations that failed to follow Christ's command.

III

A third way is open to our quest for freedom, namely, nonviolent resistance, that combines toughmindedness and tenderheartedness and avoids the complacency and do-nothingness of the softminded and the violence and bitterness of the hardhearted. My belief is that this method must guide our action in the present crisis in race relations. Through nonviolent resistance we shall be able to oppose the unjust system and at the same time love the perpetrators of the system. We must work passionately and unrelentingly for full stature as citizens, but may it never be said, my friends, that to gain it we used the inferior methods of falsehood, malice, hate, and violence.

I would not conclude without applying the meaning

of the text to the nature of God. The greatness of our God lies in the fact that he is both toughminded and tenderhearted. He has qualities both of austerity and of gentleness. The Bible, always clear in stressing both attributes of God, expresses his toughmindedness in his justice and wrath and his tenderheartedness in his love and grace. God has two outstretched arms. One is strong enough to surround us with justice, and one is gentle enough to embrace us with grace. On the one hand, God is a God of justice who punished Israel for her wayward deeds, and on the other hand, he is a forgiving father whose heart was filled with unutterable joy when the prodigal returned home.

I am thankful that we worship a God who is both toughminded and tenderhearted. If God were only toughminded, he would be a cold, passionless despot sitting in some far off heaven 'contemplating all,' as Tennyson puts it in 'The Palace of Art.' He would be Aristotle's 'unmoved mover,' self-knowing, but not other-loving.' But if God were only tenderhearted, he would be too soft and sentimental to function when things go wrong and incapable of controlling what he has made. He would be like H. G. Wells's lovable God in *God, the Invisible King,* who is strongly desirous of making a good world, but finds himself helpless before the surging powers of evil. God is neither hardhearted nor softminded. He is toughminded enough to transcend the world; he is tenderhearted enough to live in it. He does not leave us alone in our agonies and struggles. He seeks us in dark places and suffers with us and for us in our tragic prodigality.

At times we need to know that the Lord is a God of justice. When slumbering giants of injustice emerge in the earth, we need to know that there is a God of power who can cut them down like the grass and leave them withering like the green herb. When our most tireless efforts fail to stop the surging sweep of oppression, we need to know that in this universe is a God whose matchless strength is a fit contrast to the sordid weakness of man. But there are also times when we need to know that God possesses love and mercy. When we are staggered by the chilly winds of adversity and battered by the raging storms of disappointment and when through our folly and sin we stray into some destructive far country and are frustrated because of a strange feeling of homesickness, we need to know that there is Someone who loves us, cares for us, understands us, and will give us another chance. When days grow dark and nights grow dreary, we can be thankful that our God combines in his nature a creative synthesis of love and justice which will lead us through life's dark valleys and into sunlit pathways of hope and fulfillment.

Loving Your Enemies

Ye have heard that it hath been said, Thou shalt love thy neighbor, and hate thine enemy. But I say unto you, Love your enemies, bless them that curse you, do good to them that hate you, and pray for them which despitefully use you, and persecute you; that ye may be children of your Father which is in heaven.

MATTHEW 5:43–45

Probably no admonition of Jesus has been more difficult to follow than the command to 'love your enemies.' Some men have sincerely felt that its actual practice is not possible. It is easy, they say, to love those who love you, but how can one love those who openly and insidiously seek to defeat you? Others, like the philosopher Nietzsche, contend that Jesus' exhortation to love one's enemies is testimony to the fact that the Christian ethic is designed for the weak and cowardly, and not for the strong and courageous. Jesus, they say, was an impractical idealist.

In spite of these insistent questions and persistent objections, this command of Jesus challenges us with new urgency. Upheaval after upheaval has reminded us that modern man is traveling along a road called hate, in a journey that will bring us to destruction and damnation. Far from being the pious injunction of a Utopian dreamer, the command to love one's enemy is an absolute necessity for our survival. Love even for enemies is the key to the solution of the problems of our world. Jesus is not an impractical idealist: he is the practical realist.

I am certain that Jesus understood the difficulty inherent in the act of loving one's enemy. He never joined the ranks of those who talk glibly about the easiness of the moral life. He realized that every genuine expression of love grows out of a consistent and total surrender to God. So when Jesus said 'Love your enemy,' he was not unmindful of its stringent qualities. Yet he meant every word of it. Our responsibility as Christians is to discover the meaning of this command and seek passionately to live it out in our daily lives.

I

Let us be practical and ask the question, *How do we love our enemies?*

First, we must develop and maintain the capacity to forgive. He who is devoid of the power to forgive is devoid of the power to love. It is impossible even to begin the act of loving one's enemies without the prior acceptance of the necessity, over and over again, of forgiving those who inflict evil and injury upon us. It is also necessary to realize that the forgiving act must always be initiated by the person who has been wronged, the victim of some great hurt, the recipient of some tortuous injustice, the absorber of some terrible act of oppression. The wrongdoer may request forgiveness. He may come to himself, and, like the prodigal son, move up some dusty road, his heart palpitating with the desire for forgiveness. But only the injured neighbor, the loving father back home, can really pour out the warm waters of forgiveness.

Forgiveness does not mean ignoring what has been done or putting a false label on an evil act. It means, rather, that the evil act no longer remains as a barrier to the relationship. Forgiveness is a catalyst creating the atmosphere necessary for a fresh start and a new beginning. It is the lifting of a burden or the canceling of a debt. The words 'I will forgive you, but I'll never forget what you've done' never explain the real nature of forgiveness. Certainly one can never forget, if that means erasing it totally from his mind. But when we forgive, we forget in the sense that the evil deed is no longer a mental block impeding a new relationship. Likewise, we can never say, 'I will forgive you, but I won't have anything further to do with you.' Forgiveness means reconciliation, a coming together again. Without this, no man can love his enemies. The degree to which we are able to forgive determines the degree to which we are able to love our enemies.

Second, we must recognize that the evil deed of the enemy-neighbor, the thing that hurts, never quite expresses all that he is. An element of goodness may be found even in our worst enemy. Each of us is something of a schizophrenic personality, tragically divided against ourselves. A persistent civil war rages within all of our lives. Something within us causes us to lament with Ovid, the Latin poet, 'I see and approve the better things, but follow worse,' or to agree with Plato that human personality is like a charioteer having two headstrong horses, each wanting to go in a different direction, or to repeat with the Apostle Paul. 'The good that I would I do not: but the evil which I would not, that I do.'

This simply means that there is some good in the worst of us and some evil in the best of us. When we discover this, we are less prone to hate our enemies. When we look beneath the surface, beneath the impulsive evil deed, we see within our enemy-neighbor a measure of goodness and know that the viciousness and evilness of his acts are not quite representative of all that he is. We see him in a new light. We recognize that his hate grows out of fear, pride, ignorance, prejudice, and misunderstanding, but in spite of this, we know God's image is ineffably etched in his being. Then we love our enemies by realizing that they are not totally bad and that they are not beyond the reach of God's redemptive love.

Third, we must not seek to defeat or humiliate the enemy but to win his friendship and understanding. At times we are able to humiliate our worst enemy. Inevitably, his weak moments come and we are able to thrust in his side the spear of defeat. But this we must not do. Every word and deed must contribute to an understanding with the enemy and release those vast reservoirs of goodwill which have been blocked by impenetrable walls of hate.

The meaning of love is not to be confused with some sentimental outpouring. Love is something much deeper than emotional bosh. Perhaps the Greek language can clear our confusion at this point. In the Greek New Testament are three words for love. The word *eros* is a sort of aesthetic or romantic love. In the Platonic dialogues *eros* is a yearning of the soul for the realm of the divine. The second word is *philia,* a reciprocal love and the intimate affection and friendship between friends. We love those whom we like, and we love because we are loved. The third word is *agape*, understanding and creative, redemptive goodwill for all men. An overflowing love which seeks nothing in return, *agape* is the love of God operating in the human heart. At this level, we love men not because we like them, nor because their ways appeal to us, nor even because they possess some type of divine spark; we love every man because God loves him. At this level, we love the person who does an evil deed, although we hate the deed that he does.

Now we can see what Jesus meant when he said, 'Love your enemies.' We should be happy that he did not say, 'Like your enemies.' It is almost impossible to like some people. 'Like' is a sentimental and affectionate word. How can we be affectionate toward a person whose avowed aim is to crush our very being and place innumerable stumbling blocks in our path? How can we like a person who is threatening our children and bombing our homes? That is impossible. But Jesus recognized that *love* is greater than *like*. When Jesus bids us to love our enemies, he is speaking neither of *eros* nor *philia;* he is speaking of *agape,* understanding and creative, redemptive goodwill for all men. Only by following this way and responding with this type of love are we able to be children of our Father who is in heaven.

II

Let us move now from the practical *how* to the theoretical *why: Why should we love our enemies?* The first reason is fairly obvious. Returning hate for hate multiplies hate, adding deeper darkness to a night already devoid of stars. Darkness cannot drive out darkness; only light can do that. Hate cannot drive out hate; only love can do that. Hate multiplies hate, violence multiplies violence, and toughness multiplies toughness in a descending spiral of destruction. So when Jesus says 'Love your enemies,' he is setting forth a profound and ultimately inescapable admonition. Have we not come to such an impasse in the modern world that we must love our enemies – or else? The chain reaction of evil – hate begetting hate, wars producing more wars – must be broken, or we shall be plunged into the dark abyss of annihilation.

Another reason why we must love our enemies is that hate scars the soul and distorts the personality. Mindful that hate is an evil and dangerous force, we too often think of what it does to the person hated. This is understandable, for hate brings irreparable damage to its victims. We have seen its ugly consequences in the ignominious deaths brought to six million Jews by a hate-obsessed madman named Hitler, in the unspeakable violence inflicted upon Negroes by bloodthirsty mobs, in the dark horrors of war, and in the terrible indignities and injustices prepetrated against millions of God's children by unconscionable oppressors.

But there is another side which we must never overlook. Hate is just as injurious to the person who hates. Like an unchecked cancer, hate corrodes the personality and eats away its vital unity. Hate destroys a man's sense of values and his objectivity. It causes him to describe the beautiful as ugly and the ugly as beautiful, and to confuse the true with the false and the false with the true.

Dr E. Franklin Frazier, in an interesting essay entitled 'The Pathology of Race Prejudice,' included several examples of white persons who were normal, amiable, and congenial in their day-to-day relationships with other white persons but when they were challenged to think of Negroes as equals or even to discuss the question of racial injustice, they reacted with unbelievable irrationality and an abnormal unbalance. This happens when hate lingers in our minds. Psychiatrists report that many of the strange things that happen in the subconscious, many of our inner conflicts, are rooted in hate. They say, 'Love or perish.' Modern psychology recognizes what Jesus taught centuries ago: hate divides the personality and love in an amazing and inexorable way unites it.

A third reason why we should love our enemies is that love is the only force capable of transforming an enemy into a friend. We never get rid of an enemy by meeting hate with hate; we get rid of an enemy by getting rid of enmity. By its very nature, hate destroys and tears down; by its very nature, love creates and builds up. Love transforms with redemptive power.

Lincoln tried love and left for all history a magnificent drama of reconciliation. When he was campaigning for the presidency one of his arch-enemies was a man named Stanton. For some reason Stanton hated Lincoln. He used every ounce of his energy to degrade him in the eyes of the public. So deep rooted was Stanton's hate for Lincoln that he uttered unkind words about his physical appearance, and sought to embarrass him at every point with the bitterest diatribes. But in spite of this Lincoln was elected President of the United States. Then came the period when he had to select his cabinet, which would consist of the persons who would be his most intimate associates in implementing his program. He started choosing men here and there for the various secretaryships. The day finally came for Lincoln to select a man to fill the all-important post of Secretary of War. Can you imagine whom Lincoln chose to fill this post? None other than the man named Stanton. There was an immediate uproar in the inner circle when the news began to spread. Adviser after adviser was heard saying, 'Mr President, you are making a mistake. Do you know this man Stanton? Are you familiar with all of the ugly things he said about you? He is your enemy. He will seek to sabotage your program. Have you thought this through, Mr President?' Mr Lincoln's answer was terse and to the point: 'Yes, I know Mr Stanton. I am aware of all the terrible things he has said about me. But after looking over the nation, I find he is the best man for the job.' So Stanton became Abraham Lincoln's Secretary of War and rendered an invaluable service to his nation and his President. Not many years later Lincoln was assassinated. Many laudable things were said about him. Even today millions of people still adore him as the greatest of all Americans. H. G. Wells selected him as one of the six great men of history. But of all the great statements made about Abraham Lincoln, the words of Stanton remain among the greatest. Standing near the dead body of the man he once hated, Stanton referred to him as one of the greatest men that ever lived and said 'he now belongs to the ages.' If Lincoln had hated Stanton both men would have gone to their graves as bitter enemies. But through the power of love Lincoln transformed an enemy into a friend. It was this same attitude that made it possible for Lincoln to speak a kind word about the South during the Civil War when feeling was most bitter. Asked by a shocked bystander how he could do this, Lincoln said, 'Madam, do I not destroy my enemies when I make them my friends?' This is the power of redemptive love.

We must hasten to say that these are not the ultimate reasons why we should love our enemies. An even more basic reason why we are commanded to love is expressed explicitly in Jesus' words, 'Love your enemies . . . *that ye may be children of your Father which is in heaven.*' We are called to this difficult task in order to realize a unique relationship with God. We are potential sons of God. Through love that potentiality becomes actuality. We must love our enemies, because only by loving them can we know God and experience the beauty of his holiness.

The relevance of what I have said to the crisis in race relations should be readily apparent. There will be no permanent solution to the race problem until oppressed men develop the capacity to love their enemies. The darkness of racial injustice will be dispelled only by the light of forgiving love. For more than three centuries American Negroes have been battered by the iron rod of oppression, frustrated by day and bewildered by night by unbearable injustice, and burdened with the ugly weight of discrimination. Forced to live with these shameful conditions, we are tempted to become bitter and to retaliate with a corresponding hate. But if this happens, the new order we seek will be little more than a duplicate of the old order. We must in strength and humility meet hate with love.

Of course, this is not *practical*. Life is a matter of getting even, of hitting back, of dog eat dog. Am I saying that Jesus commands us to love those who hurt and oppress us? Do I sound like most preachers – idealistic and impractical? Maybe in some distant Utopia, you say, that idea will work, but not in the hard, cold world in which we live.

My friends, we have followed the so-called practical way for too long a time now, and it has led inexorably to deeper confusion and chaos. Time is cluttered with the wreckage of communities which surrendered to hatred and violence. For the salvation of our nation and the salvation of mankind, we must follow another way. This does not mean that we abandon our righteous efforts. With every ounce of our energy we must continue to rid this nation of the incubus of segregation. But we shall not in the process relinquish our privilege and our obligation to love. While abhorring segregation, we shall love the segregationist. This is the only way to create the beloved community.

To our most bitter opponents we say: 'We shall match your capacity to inflict suffering by our capacity to endure suffering. We shall meet your physical force with soul force. Do to us what you will, and we shall continue to love you. We cannot in all good conscience obey your unjust laws, because noncooperation with evil is as much a moral obligation as is cooperation with good. Throw us in jail, and we shall still love you. Send your hooded perpetrators of violence into our community at the midnight hour and beat us and leave us half dead, and we shall still love you. But be ye assured that we will wear you down by our capacity to suffer. One day we shall win freedom, but not only for ourselves.

We shall so appeal to your heart and conscience that we shall win *you* in the process, and our victory will be a double victory.'

Love is the most durable power in the world. This creative force, so beautifully exemplified in the life of our Christ, is the most potent instrument available in mankind's quest for peace and security. Napoleon Bonaparte, the great military genius, looking back over his years of conquest, is reported to have said: 'Alexander, Caesar, Charlemagne and I have built great empires. But upon what did they depend? They depended on force. But centuries ago Jesus started an empire that was built on love, and even to this day millions will die for him.' Who can doubt the veracity of these words? The great military leaders of the past have gone, and their empires have crumbled and burned to ashes. But the empire of Jesus, built solidly and majestically on the foundation of love, is still growing. It started with a small group of dedicated men, who, through the inspiration of their Lord, were able to shake the hinges from the gates of the Roman Empire, and carry the gospel into all the world. Today the vast earthly kingdom of Christ numbers more than 900,000,000 and covers every land and tribe. Today we hear again the promise of victory:

> *Jesus shall reign where'er the sun*
> *Does his successive journeys run;*
> *His kingdom stretch from shore to shore,*
> *Till moons shall wax and wane no more.*

Another choir joyously responds:

> *In Christ there is no East or West,*
> *In Him no South or North,*
> *But one great Fellowship of Love*
> *Throughout the whole wide earth.*

Jesus is eternally right. History is replete with the bleached bones of nations that refused to listen to him. May we in the twentieth century hear and follow his words – before it is too late. May we solemnly realize that we shall never be true sons of our heavenly Father until we love our enemies and pray for those who persecute us.

Pilgrimage to Nonviolence

In my senior year in theological seminary, I engaged in the exciting reading of various theological theories. Having been raised in a rather strict fundamentalist tradition, I was occasionally shocked when my intellectual journey carried me through new and sometimes complex doctrinal lands, but the pilgrimage was always stimulating, gave me a new appreciation for objective appraisal and critical analysis, and knocked me out of my dogmatic slumber.

Liberalism provided me with an intellectual satisfaction that I had never found in fundamentalism. I became so enamored of the insights of liberalism that I almost fell into the trap of accepting uncritically everything it encompassed. I was absolutely convinced of the natural goodness of man and the natural power of human reason.

I

A basic change in my thinking came when I began to question some of the theories that had been associated with so-called liberal theology. Of course, there are aspects of liberalism that I hope to cherish always: its devotion to the search for truth, its insistence on an open and analytical mind, and its refusal to abandon the best lights of reason. The contribution of liberalism to the philological-historical criticism of biblical literature has been of immeasurable value and should be defended with religious and scientific passion.

But I began to question the liberal doctrine of man. The more I observed the tragedies of history and man's shameful inclination to choose the low road, the more I came to see the depths and strength of sin. My reading of the works of Reinhold Niebuhr made me aware of the complexity of human motives and the reality of sin on every level of man's existence. Moreover, I came to recognize the complexity of man's social involvement and the glaring reality of collective evil. I realized that liberalism had been all too sentimental concerning human nature and that it leaned toward a false idealism.

I also came to see that the superficial optimism of liberalism concerning human nature overlooked the fact that reason is darkened by sin. The more I thought about human nature, the more I saw how our tragic inclination for sin encourages us to rationalize our actions. Liberalism failed to show that reason by itself is little more than an instrument to justify man's defensive ways of thinking. Reason, devoid of the purifying power of faith, can never free itself from distortions and rationalizations.

Although I rejected some aspects of liberalism, I never came to an all-out acceptance of neo-orthodoxy. While I saw neo-orthodoxy as a helpful corrective for a sentimental liberalism, I felt that it did not provide an adequate answer to basic questions. If liberalism was too optimistic concerning human nature, neo-orthodoxy was too pessimistic. Not only on the question of man, but also on other vital issues, the revolt of neo-orthodoxy went too far. In its attempt to preserve the transcendence of God, which had been neglected by an overstress of his immanence in liberalism, neo-orthodoxy went to the extreme of stressing a God who was hidden, unknown, and 'wholly other.' In its revolt against overemphasis on the power of reason in liberalism, neo-orthodoxy fell into a mood of antirationalism and semifundamentalism, stressing a narrow uncritical biblicism. This approach, I felt, was inadequate both for the church and for personal life.

So although liberalism left me unsatisfied on the question of the nature of man, I found no refuge in neo-orthodoxy. I am now convinced that the truth about man is found neither in liberalism nor in neo-orthodoxy. Each represents a partial truth. A large segment of Protestant liberalism defined man only in terms of his essential nature, his capacity for good; neo-orthodoxy tended to define man only in terms of his existential nature, his capacity for evil. An adequate understanding of man is found neither in the thesis of liberalism nor in the antithesis of neo-orthodoxy, but in a synthesis which reconciles the truths of both.

During the intervening years I have gained a new appreciation for the philosophy of existentialism. My first contact with this philosophy came through my reading of Kierkegaard and Nietzsche. Later I turned to a study of Jaspers, Heidegger, and Sartre. These thinkers stimulated my thinking; while questioning each, I nevertheless learned a great deal through a study of them. When I finally engaged in a serious study of the writings of Paul Tillich, I became convinced that existentialism, in spite of the fact that it had become all too fashionable, had grasped certain basic truths about man and his condition that could not be permanently overlooked.

An understanding of the 'finite freedom' of man is one of the permanent contributions of existentialism, and its perception of the anxiety and conflict produced in man's personal and social life by the perilous and ambiguous structure of existence is especially meaningful for our time. A common denominator in atheistic or theistic existentialism is that man's existential situation is estranged from his essential nature. In their revolt against Hegel's essentialism, all existentialists contend that the world is fragmented. History is a series of unreconciled conflicts, and man's existence is filled with anxiety and threatened with meaninglessness. While the ultimate Christian answer is not found in any of these existential assertions, there is much here by which the theologian may describe the true state of man's existence.

Although most of my formal study has been in systematic theology and philosophy, I have become more and more interested in social ethics. During my early teens I was deeply concerned by the problem of racial

injustice. I considered segregation both rationally inex-
plicable and morally unjustifiable. I could never accept
my having to sit in the back of a bus or in the segregated
section of a train. The first time that I was seated behind
a curtain in a dining-car I felt as though the curtain had
been dropped on my selfhood. I also learned that the
inseparable twin of racial injustice is economic injustice.
I saw how the systems of segregation exploited both the
Negro and the poor whites. These early experiences
made me deeply conscious of the varieties of injustice
in our society.

II

Not until I entered theological seminary, however, did
I begin a serious intellectual quest for a method that
would eliminate social evil. I was immediately influ-
enced by the social gospel. In the early 1950s I read
Walter Rauschenbusch's *Christianity and the Social
Crisis*, a book which left an indelible imprint on my
thinking. Of course, there were points at which I dif-
fered with Rauschenbusch. I felt that he was a victim of
the nineteenth-century 'cult of inevitable progress,'
which led him to an unwarranted optimism concerning
human nature. Moreover, he came perilously close to
identifying the Kingdom of God with a particular social
and economic system, a temptation to which the church
must never surrender. But in spite of these shortcom-
ings, Rauschenbusch gave to American Protestantism a
sense of social responsibility that it should never lose.

The gospel at its best deals with the whole man, not only his soul but also his body, not only his spiritual well-being but also his material well-being. A religion that professes a concern for the souls of men and is not equally concerned about the slums that damn them, the economic conditions that strangle them, and the social conditions that cripple them, is a spiritually moribund religion.

After reading Rauschenbusch, I turned to a serious study of the social and ethical theories of the great philosophers. During this period I had almost despaired of the power of love to solve social problems. The turn-the-other-cheek and the love-your-enemies philosophies are valid, I felt, only when individuals are in conflict with other individuals; when racial groups and nations are in conflict, a more realistic approach is necessary.

Then I was introduced to the life and teachings of Mahatma Gandhi. As I read his works I became deeply fascinated by his campaigns of nonviolent resistance. The whole Gandhian concept of *satyagraha* (*satya* is truth which equals love and *graha* is force; *satyagraha* thus means truth-force or love-force) was profoundly significant to me. As I delved deeper into the philosophy of Gandhi, my scepticism concerning the power of love gradually diminished, and I came to see for the first time that the Christian doctrine of love, operating through the Gandhian method of nonviolence, is one of the most potent weapons available to an oppressed people in their struggle for freedom. At that time, however, I acquired only an intellectual understanding and appreciation of the position, and I had no firm determination to organize it in a socially effective situation.

When I was in Montgomery, Alabama, as a pastor in 1954, I had not the slightest idea that I would later become involved in a crisis in which nonviolent resistance would be applicable. After I had lived in the community about a year, the bus boycott began. The Negro people of Montgomery, exhausted by the humiliating experiences that they had constantly faced on the buses, expressed in a massive act of non-cooperation their determination to be free. They came to see that it was ultimately more honorable to walk the streets in dignity than to ride the buses in humiliation. At the beginning of the protest, the people called on me to serve as their spokesman. In accepting this responsibility, my mind, consciously or unconsciously, was driven back to the Sermon on the Mount and the Gandhian method of nonviolent resistance. This principle became the guiding light of our movement. Christ furnished the spirit and motivation and Gandhi furnished the method.

The experience in Montgomery did more to clarify my thinking in regard to the question of nonviolence than all of the books that I had read. As the days unfolded, I became more and more convinced of the power of nonviolence. Nonviolence became more than a method to which I gave intellectual assent; it became a commitment to a way of life. Many issues I had not cleared up intellectually concerning nonviolence were now resolved within the sphere of practical action.

My privilege of traveling to India had a great impact

on me personally, for it was invigorating to see firsthand the amazing results of a nonviolent struggle to achieve independence. The aftermath of hatred and bitterness that usually follows a violent campaign was found nowhere in India, and a mutual friendship, based on complete equality, existed between the Indian and British people within the Commonwealth.

I would not wish to give the impression that nonviolence will accomplish miracles overnight. Men are not easily moved from their mental ruts or purged of their prejudiced and irrational feelings. When the underprivileged demand freedom, the privileged at first react with bitterness and resistance. Even when the demands are couched in nonviolent terms, the initial response is substantially the same. I am sure that many of our white brothers in Montgomery and throughout the South are still bitter toward the Negro leaders, even though these leaders have sought to follow a way of love and nonviolence. But the nonviolent approach does something to the hearts and souls of those committed to it. It gives them new self-respect. It calls up resources of strength and courage that they did not know they had. Finally, it so stirs the conscience of the opponent that reconciliation becomes a reality.

III

More recently I have come to see the need for the method of nonviolence in international relations. Although I was not yet convinced of its efficacy in conflicts between nations, I felt that while war could never be a positive good, it could serve as a negative good by preventing the spread and growth of an evil force. War, horrible as it is, might be preferable to surrender to a totalitarian system. But I now believe that the potential destructiveness of modern weapons totally rules out the possibility of war ever again achieving a negative good. If we assume that mankind has a right to survive, then we must find an alternative to war and destruction. In our day of space vehicles and guided ballistic missiles, the choice is either nonviolence or nonexistence.

I am no doctrinaire pacifist, but I have tried to embrace a realistic pacifism which finds the pacifist position as the lesser evil in the circumstances. I do not claim to be free from the moral dilemmas that the Christian nonpacifist confronts, but I am convinced that the church cannot be silent while mankind faces the threat of nuclear annihilation. If the church is true to her mission, she must call for an end to the arms race.

Some of my personal sufferings over the last few years have also served to shape my thinking. I always hesitate to mention these experiences for fear of conveying the wrong impression. A person who constantly calls attention to his trials and sufferings is in danger of developing a martyr complex and impressing others that he is consciously seeking sympathy. It is possible for one to be self-centered in his self-sacrifice. But I feel somewhat justified in mentioning them in this essay because of the influence they have had upon my thought.

Due to my involvement in the struggle for the freedom of my people, I have been imprisoned in Alabama and Georgia jails twelve times. My home has been bombed twice. A day seldom passes that my family and I are not the recipients of threats of death. I have been the victim of a near-fatal stabbing. So in a real sense I have been battered by the storms of persecution. I must admit that at times I have felt that I could no longer bear such a heavy burden, and have been tempted to retreat to a more quiet and serene life. But every time such a temptation appeared, something came to strengthen and sustain my determination. I have learned now that the Master's burden is light precisely when we take his yoke upon us.

My personal trials have also taught me the value of unmerited suffering. As my sufferings mounted I soon realized that there were two ways in which I could respond to my situation – either to react with bitterness or seek to transform the suffering into a creative force. I decided to follow the latter course. Recognizing the necessity for suffering, I have tried to make of it a virtue. If only to save myself from bitterness, I have attempted to see my personal ordeals as an opportunity to transfigure myself and heal the people involved in the tragic situation which now obtains. I have lived these last few years with the conviction that unearned suffering is redemptive. There are some who still find the cross a stumbling block, others consider it foolishness, but I am more convinced than ever before that it is the power of God unto social and individual salvation. So like the

Apostle Paul I can now humbly, yet proudly, say, 'I bear in my body the marks of the Lord Jesus.'

The agonizing moments through which I have passed during the last few years have also drawn me closer to God. More than ever before I am convinced of the reality of a personal God. True, I have always believed in the personality of God. But in the past the idea of a personal God was little more than a metaphysical category that I found theologically and philosophically satisfying. Now it is a living reality that has been validated in the experiences of everyday life. God has been profoundly real to me in recent years. In the midst of outer dangers I have felt an inner calm. In the midst of lonely days and dreary nights I have heard an inner voice saying, 'Lo, I will be with you.' When the chains of fear and the manacles of frustration have all but stymied my efforts, I have felt the power of God transforming the fatigue of despair into the buoyancy of hope. I am convinced that the universe is under the control of a loving purpose, and that in the struggle for righteousness man has cosmic companionship. Behind the harsh appearances of the world there is a benign power. To say that this God is personal is not to make him a finite object besides other objects or attribute to him the limitations of human personality; it is to take what is finest and noblest in our consciousness and affirm its perfect existence in him. It is certainly true that human personality is limited, but personality as such involves no necessary limitations. It means simply self-consciousness and self-direction. So in the truest sense of the word, God is a living God. In him there is feeling and will, responsive to the deepest yearnings of the human heart: *this* God both evokes and answers prayer.

The past decade has been a most exciting one. In spite of the tensions and uncertainties of this period something profoundly meaningful is taking place. Old systems of exploitation and oppression are passing away; new systems of justice and equality are being born. In a real sense this is a great time to be alive. Therefore, I am not yet discouraged about the future. Granted that the easygoing optimism of yesterday is impossible. Granted that we face a world crisis which leaves us standing so often amid the surging murmur of life's restless sea. But every crisis has both its dangers and its opportunities. It can spell either salvation or doom. In a dark, confused world the Kingdom of God may yet reign in the hearts of men.

The Negro Revolution – Why 1963?

The bitterly cold winter of 1962 lingered throughout the opening months of 1963, touching the land with chill and frost, and then was replaced by a placid spring. Americans awaited a quiet summer. That it would be pleasant they had no doubt. The worst of it would be the nightmare created by sixty million cars, all apparently trying to reach the same destination at the same time. Fifty million families looked forward to the pleasure of two hundred million vacations in the American tradition of the frenetic hunt for relaxation.

It would be a pleasant summer because, in the mind of the average man, there was little cause for concern. The blithe outlook about the state of the nation was reflected from as high up as the White House. The administration confidently readied a tax-reduction bill. Business and employment were at comfortable levels. Money was – for many Americans – plentiful.

Summer came, and the weather was beautiful. But the climate, the social climate of American life, erupted into lightning flashes, trembled with thunder and vibrated to the relentless, growing rain of protest come to life through the land. Explosively, America's third revolution – the Negro Revolution – had begun.

For the first time in the long and turbulent history of the nation, almost one thousand cities were engulfed in civil turmoil, with violence trembling just below the surface. Reminiscent of the French Revolution of 1789, the streets had become a battleground, just as they had become the battleground, in the 1830s, of England's tumultuous Chartist movement. As in these two revolutions, a submerged social group, propelled by a burning need for justice, lifting itself with sudden swiftness, moving with determination and a majestic scorn for risk and danger, created an uprising so powerful that it shook a huge society from its comfortable base.

Never in American history had a group seized the streets, the squares, the sacrosanct business thoroughfares and the marbled halls of government to protest and proclaim the unendurability of their oppression. Had room-size machines turned human, burst from the plants that housed them and stalked the land in revolt, the nation could not have been more amazed. Undeniably, the Negro had been an object of sympathy and wore the scars of deep grievances, but the nation had come to count on him as a creature who could quietly endure, silently suffer and patiently wait. He was well trained in service and, whatever the provocation, he neither pushed back nor spoke back.

Just as lightning makes no sound until it strikes, the Negro Revolution generated quietly. But when it struck, the revealing flash of its power and the impact of its sincerity and fervor displayed a force of a frightening intensity. Three hundred years of humiliation, abuse and deprivation cannot be expected to find voice in a whisper. The storm clouds did not release a 'gentle rain from heaven,' but a whirlwind, which has not yet spent its force or attained its full momentum.

Because there is more to come; because American society is bewildered by the spectacle of the Negro in revolt; because the dimensions are vast and the implications deep in a nation with twenty million Negroes, it is important to understand the history that is being made today.

II

Some years ago, I sat in a Harlem department store, surrounded by hundreds of people. I was autographing copies of *Stride Toward Freedom*, my book about the Montgomery bus boycott of 1955–56. As I signed my name to a page, I felt something sharp plunge forcefully into my chest. I had been stabbed with a letter opener, struck home by a woman who would later be judged insane. Rushed by ambulance to Harlem Hospital, I lay in a bed for hours while preparations were made to remove the keen-edged knife from my body. Days later, when I was well enough to talk with Dr. Aubrey Maynard, the chief of the surgeons who performed the delicate, dangerous operation, I learned the reason for the long delay that preceded surgery. He told me that the razor tip of the instrument had been touching my aorta and that my whole chest had to be opened to extract it.

'If you had sneezed during all those hours of waiting,' Dr Maynard said, 'your aorta would have been punctured and you would have drowned in your own blood.'

In the summer of 1963 the knife of violence was just that close to the nation's aorta. Hundreds of cities might now be mourning countless dead but for the operation of certain forces which gave political surgeons an opportunity to cut boldly and safely to remove the deadly peril.

What was it that gave us the second chance? To answer this we must answer another question. Why did this Revolution occur in 1963? Negroes had for decades endured evil. In the words of the poet, they had long asked: 'Why must the blackness of nighttime collect in our mouth; why must we always taste grief in our blood?' Any time would seem to have been the right time. Why 1963?

Why did a thousand cities shudder almost simultaneously and why did the whole world – in gleaming capitals and mud-hut villages – hold its breath during those months? Why was it this year that the American Negro, so long ignored, so long written out of the pages of history books, tramped a declaration of freedom with his marching feet across the pages of newspapers, the television screens and the magazines? Sarah Turner closed the kitchen cupboard and went into the streets; John Wilkins shut down the elevator and enlisted in the nonviolent army; Bill Griggs slammed the brakes of his truck and slid to the sidewalk; the Reverend Arthur Jones led his flock into the streets and held church in jail.

The words and actions of parliaments and statesmen, of kings and prime ministers, movie stars and athletes, were shifted from the front pages to make room for the history-making deeds of the servants, the drivers, the elevator operators and the ministers. Why in 1963, and what has this to do with why the dark threat of violence did not erupt in blood?

III

The Negro had been deeply disappointed over the slow pace of school desegregation. He knew that in 1954 the highest court in the land had handed down a decree calling for desegregation of schools 'with all deliberate speed.' He knew that this edict from the Supreme Court had been heeded with all deliberate delay. At the beginning of 1963, nine years after this historic decision, approximately 9 percent of southern Negro students were attending integrated schools. If this pace were maintained, it would be the year 2054 before integration in southern schools would be a reality.

In its wording the Supreme Court decision had revealed an awareness that attempts would be made to evade its intent. The phrase 'all deliberate speed' did not mean that another century should be allowed to unfold before we released Negro children from the narrow pigeonhole of the segregated schools; it meant that, giving some courtesy and consideration to the need for softening old attitudes and outdated customs, democracy must press ahead, out of the past of ignorance and

intolerance, and into the present of educational opportunity and moral freedom.

Yet the statistics make it abundantly clear that the
segregationists of the South remained undefeated by
the decision. From every section of Dixie, the announce-
ment of the high court had been met with declarations
of defiance. Once recovered from their initial outrage,
these defenders of the status quo had seized the offensive to impose their own schedule of change. The progress
that was supposed to have been achieved with deliberate speed had created change for less than 2 percent of
Negro children in most areas of the South and not even
one-tenth of 1 percent in some parts of the deepest
South.

There was another factor in the slow pace of progress, a factor of which few are aware and even fewer
understand. It is an unadvertised fact that soon after the
1954 decision the Supreme Court retreated from its own
position by giving approval to the Pupil Placement Law.
This law permitted the states themselves to determine
where school children might be placed by virtue of family background, special ability and other subjective
criteria. The Pupil Placement Law was almost as far-
reaching in modifying and limiting the integration of
schools as the original decision had been in attempting
to eliminate segregation. Without technically reversing
itself, the Court had granted legal sanction to tokenism
and thereby guaranteed that segregation, in substance,
would last for an indefinite period, though formally it
was illegal.

In order, then, to understand the deep disillusion of the Negro in 1963, one must examine his contrasting emotions at the time of the decision and during the nine years that followed. One must understand the pendulum swing between the elation that arose when the edict was handed down and the despair that followed the failure to bring it to life.

A second reason for the outburst in 1963 was rooted in disappointment with both political parties. From the city of Los Angeles in 1960, the Democratic party had written an historic and sweeping civil-rights pronouncement into its campaign platform. The Democratic standard bearer had repeated eloquently and often that the moral weight of the presidency must be applied to this burning issue. From Chicago, the Republican party had been generous in its convention vows on civil rights, although its candidate had made no great effort in his campaign to convince the nation that he would redeem his party's promises.

Then 1961 and 1962 arrived, with both parties marking time in the cause of justice. In the Congress, reactionary Republicans were still doing business with the Dixiecrats. And the feeling was growing among Negroes that the administration had oversimplified and underestimated the civil-rights issue. President Kennedy, if not backing down, had backed away from a key pledge of his campaign – to wipe out housing discrimination immediately 'with the stroke of a pen.' When he had finally signed the housing order, two years after taking office, its terms, though praiseworthy, had revealed a serious weakness in its failure to attack the key problem of discrimination in financing by banks and other institutions.

While Negroes were being appointed to some significant jobs, and social hospitality was being extended at the White House to Negro leaders, the dreams of the masses remained in tatters. The Negro felt that he recognized the same old bone that had been tossed to him in the past – only now it was being handed to him on a platter, with courtesy.

The administration had fashioned its primary approach to discrimination in the South around a series of lawsuits chiefly designed to protect the right to vote. Opposition toward action on other fronts had begun to harden. With each new Negro protest, we were advised, sometimes privately and sometimes in public, to call off our efforts and channel all of our energies into registering voters. On each occasion we would agree with the importance of voting rights, but would patiently seek to explain that Negroes did not want to neglect all other rights while one was selected for concentrated attention.

It was necessary to conclude that our argument was not persuading the administration any more than the government's logic was prevailing with us. Negroes had manifested their faith by racking up a substantial majority of their votes for President Kennedy. They had expected more of him than of the previous administration. In no sense had President Kennedy betrayed his promises. Yet his administration appeared to believe it was doing as much as was politically possible and had, by its positive deeds, earned enough credit to coast on civil rights. Politically, perhaps, this was not a surprising conclusion. How many people understood, during the first two years of the Kennedy administration, that the Negroes' 'Now' was becoming as militant as the segregationists' 'Never'? Eventually the president would set political considerations aside and rise to the level of his own unswerving moral commitment. But this was still in the future.

No discussion of the influences that bore on the thinking of the Negro in 1963 would be complete without some attention to the relationship of this Revolution to international events. Throughout the upheavals of cold-war politics, Negroes had seen their government go to the brink of nuclear conflict more than once. The justification for risking the annihilation of the human race was always expressed in terms of America's willingness to go to any lengths to preserve freedom. To the Negro that readiness for heroic measures in the defense of liberty disappeared or became tragically weak when the threat was within our own borders and was concerned with the Negro's liberty. While the Negro is not so selfish as to stand isolated in concern for his own dilemma, ignoring the ebb and flow of events around the world, there is a certain bitter irony in the picture of his country championing freedom in foreign lands and failing to ensure that freedom to twenty million of its own.

From beyond the borders of his own land, the Negro had been inspired by another powerful force. He had watched the decolonization and liberation of nations in Africa and Asia since World War II. He knew that yellow, black and brown people had felt for years that the American Negro was too passive, unwilling to take strong measures to gain his freedom. He might have remembered the visit to this country of an African head of state, who was called upon by a delegation of prominent American Negroes. When they began reciting to him their long list of grievances, the visiting statesman had waved a weary hand and said:

'I am aware of current events. I know everything you are telling me about what the white man is doing to the Negro. Now tell me: What is the Negro doing for himself?'

The American Negro saw, in the land from which he had been snatched and thrown into slavery, a great pageant of political progress. He realized that just thirty years ago there were only three independent nations in the whole of Africa. He knew that by 1963 more than thirty-four African nations had risen from colonial bondage. The Negro saw black statesmen voting on vital issues in the United Nations – and knew that in many cities of his own land he was not permitted to take that significant walk to the ballot box. He saw black kings and potentates ruling from palaces – and knew he had been condemned to move from small ghettos to larger ones. Witnessing the drama of Negro progress elsewhere in the world, witnessing a level of conspicuous consumption at home exceeding anything in our history, it was natural that by 1963 Negroes would rise with resolution and demand a share of governing power, and living conditions measured by American standards rather than by the standards of colonial impoverishment.

An additional and decisive fact confronted the Negro and helped to bring him out of the houses, into the streets, out of the trenches and into the front lines. This was his recognition that one hundred years had passed since emancipation, with no profound effect on his plight.

With the dawn of 1963, plans were afoot all over the land to celebrate the Emancipation Proclamation, the one-hundredth birthday of the Negro's liberation from bondage. In Washington, a federal commission had been established to mark the event. Governors of states and mayors of cities had utilized the date to enhance their political image by naming commissions, receiving committees, issuing statements, planning state pageants, sponsoring dinners, endorsing social activities. Champagne, this year, would bubble on countless tables. Appropriately attired, over thick cuts of roast beef, legions would listen as luminous phrases were spun to salute the great democratic landmark which 1963 represented.

But alas! All the talk and publicity accompanying the centennial only served to remind the Negro that he still wasn't free, that he still lived a form of slavery disguised by certain niceties of complexity. As the then vice president, Lyndon B. Johnson, phrased it: 'Emancipation was a Proclamation but not a fact.' The pen of the Great

Emancipator had moved the Negro into the sunlight of physical freedom, but actual conditions had left him behind in the shadow of political, psychological, social, economic and intellectual bondage. In the South, discrimination faced the Negro in its obvious and glaring forms. In the North, it confronted him in hidden and subtle disguise.

The Negro also had to recognize that one hundred years after emancipation he lived on a lonely island of economic insecurity in the midst of a vast ocean of material prosperity. Negroes are still at the bottom of the economic ladder. They live within two concentric circles of segregation. One imprisons them on the basis of color, while the other confines them within a separate culture of poverty. The average Negro is born into want and deprivation. His struggle to escape his circumstances is hindered by color discrimination. He is deprived of normal education and normal social and economic opportunities. When he seeks opportunity, he is told, in effect, to lift himself by his own bootstraps, advice which does not take into account the fact that he is barefoot.

By 1963, most of America's working population had forgotten the Great Depression or had never known it. The slow and steady growth of unemployment had touched some of the white working force but the proportion was still not more than one in twenty. This was not true for the Negro. There were two and one-half times as many jobless Negroes as whites in 1963, and their median income was half that of the white man.

Many white Americans of good will have never connected bigotry with economic exploitation. They have deplored prejudice, but tolerated or ignored economic injustice. But the Negro knows that these two evils have a malignant kinship. He knows this because he has worked in shops that employ him exclusively because the pay is below a living standard. He knows it is not an accident of geography that wage rates in the South are significantly lower than those in the North. He knows that the spotlight recently focused on the growth in the number of women who work is not a phenomenon in Negro life. The average Negro woman has always had to work to help keep her family in food and clothes.

To the Negro, as 1963 approached, the economic structure of society appeared to be so ordered that a precise sifting of jobs took place. The lowest-paid employment and the most tentative jobs were reserved for him. If he sought to change his position, he was walled in by the tall barrier of discrimination. As summer came, more than ever the spread of unemployment had visible and tangible dimensions to the colored American. Equality meant dignity and dignity demanded a job that was secure and a paycheck that lasted throughout the week.

The Negro's economic problem was compounded by the emergence and growth of automation. Since discrimination and lack of education confined him to unskilled and semi-skilled labor, the Negro was and remains the first to suffer in these days of great technological development. The Negro knew all too well that there was not in existence the kind of vigorous retraining program that could really help him to grapple with the magnitude of his problem.

The symbol of the job beyond the great wall was construction work. The Negro whose slave labor helped to build a nation was being told by employers on the one hand and unions on the other that there was no place for him in this industry. Billions were being spent on city, state and national building for which the Negro paid taxes but could draw no paycheck. No one who saw the spanning bridges, the grand mansions, the sturdy docks and stout factories of the South could question the Negro's ability to build if he were given a chance for apprenticeship training. It was plain, hard, raw discrimination that shut him out of decent employment.

In 1963, the Negro, who had realized for many years that he was not truly free, awoke from a stupor of inaction with the cold dash of realization that 1963 meant one hundred years after Lincoln gave his autograph to the cause of freedom.

The milestone of the centennial of emancipation gave the Negro a reason to act – a reason so simple and obvious that he almost had to step back to see it.

Simple logic made it painfully clear that if this centennial were to be meaningful, it must be observed not as a celebration, but rather as a commemoration of the one moment in the country's history when a bold, brave *start* had been made, and a rededication to the obvious fact that urgent business was at hand – the resumption of that noble journey toward the goals reflected in the Preamble to the Constitution, the Constitution itself, the Bill of Rights and the Thirteenth, Fourteenth and Fifteenth Amendments.

Yet not all of these forces conjoined could have brought about the massive and largely bloodless Revolution of 1963 if there had not been at hand a philosophy and a method worthy of its goals. Nonviolent direct action did not originate in America, but it found its natural home in this land, where refusal to cooperate with injustice was an ancient and honorable tradition and where Christian forgiveness was written into the minds and hearts of good men. Tested in Montgomery during the winter of 1955–56, and toughened throughout the South in the eight ensuing years, nonviolent resistance had become, by 1963, the logical force in the greatest mass-action crusade for freedom that has ever occurred in American history.

Nonviolence is a powerful and just weapon. It is a weapon unique in history, which cuts without wounding and ennobles the man who wields it. It is a sword that heals. Both a practical and a moral answer to the Negro's cry for justice, nonviolent direct action proved that it could win victories without losing wars, and so became the triumphant tactic of the Negro Revolution of 1963.

The Sword That Heals

In the summer of 1963 a need and a time and a circumstance and the mood of a people came together. In order to understand the present Revolution, it is necessary to examine in more extensive detail the psychological and social conditions that produced it and the events that brought the philosophy and method of nonviolent direct action into the forefront of the struggle.

It is important to understand, first of all, that the Revolution is not indicative of a sudden loss of patience within the Negro. The Negro had never really been patient in the pure sense of the word. The posture of silent waiting was forced upon him psychologically because he was shackled physically.

In the days of slavery, this suppression was openly, scientifically and consistently applied. Sheer physical force kept the Negro captive at every point. He was prevented from learning to read and write, prevented by laws actually inscribed in the statute books. He was forbidden to associate with other Negroes living on the same plantation, except when weddings or funerals took place. Punishment for any form of resistance or complaint about his condition could range from mutilation to death. Families were torn apart, friends separated, cooperation to improve their condition carefully thwarted. Fathers and mothers were sold from their children and children were bargained away from their parents. Young girls were, in many cases, sold to become the breeders of fresh generations of slaves. The slaveholders of America had devised with almost scientific precision their systems for keeping the Negro defenseless, emotionally and physically.

With the ending of physical slavery after the Civil War, new devices were found to 'keep the Negro in his place.' It would take volumes to describe these methods, extending from birth in jim-crow hospitals through burial in jim-crow sections of cemeteries. They are too well known to require a catalogue here. Yet one of the revelations during the past few years is the fact that the straitjackets of race prejudice and discrimination do not wear only southern labels. The subtle, psychological technique of the North has approached in its ugliness and victimization of the Negro the outright terror and open brutality of the South. The result has been a demeanor that passed for patience in the eyes of the white man, but covered a powerful impatience in the heart of the Negro.

For years, in the South, the white segregationist has been saying the Negro was 'satisfied.' He has claimed 'we get along beautifully with our Negroes because we understand them. We only have trouble when outside agitators come in and stir it up.' Many expressed this point of view knowing that it was a lie of majestic proportions. Others believed they were speaking the truth.

For corroboration, they would tell you: 'Why, I talked to my cook and she said . . .' or, 'I discussed this frankly with the colored boy who works for us and I told him to express himself freely. He said . . .'

White people in the South may never fully know the extent to which Negroes defended themselves and protected their jobs – and, in many cases, their lives – by perfecting an air of ignorance and agreement. In days gone by, no cook would have dared to tell her employer what he ought to know. She had to tell him what he wanted to hear. She knew that the penalty for speaking the truth could be loss of her job.

During the Montgomery bus boycott, a white family summoned their Negro cook and asked her if she supported the terrible things the Negroes were doing, boycotting buses and demanding jobs.

'Oh, no, ma'am, I won't have anything to do with that boycott thing,' the cook said. 'I am just going to stay away from the buses as long as that trouble is going on.' No doubt she left a satisfied audience. But as she walked home from her job, on feet already weary from a full day's work, she walked proudly, knowing that she was marching with a movement that would bring into being nonsegregated bus travel in Montgomery.

Jailing the Negro was once as much of a threat as the loss of a job. To any Negro who displayed a spark of manhood, a southern law-enforcement officer could say: 'Nigger, watch your step, or I'll put you in jail.' The Negro knew what going to jail meant. It meant not only confinement and isolation from his loved ones. It meant that at the jailhouse he could probably expect a severe beating. And it meant that his day in court, if he had it, would be a mockery of justice.

Even today there still exists in the South – and in certain areas of the North – the license that our society allows to unjust officials who implement their authority in the name of justice to practice injustice against minorities. Where, in the days of slavery, social license and custom placed the unbridled power of the whip in the hands of overseers and masters, today – especially in the southern half of the nation – armies of officials are clothed in uniform, invested with authority, armed with the instruments of violence and death and conditioned to believe that they can intimidate, maim or kill Negroes with the same recklessness that once motivated the slaveowner. If one doubts this conclusion, let him search the records and find how rarely in any southern state a police officer has been punished for abusing a Negro.

Since nonviolent action has entered the scene, however, the white man has gasped at a new phenomenon. He has seen Negroes, by the hundreds and by the thousands, marching toward him, knowing they are going to jail, wanting to go to jail, willing to accept the confinement, willing to risk the beatings and the uncertain justice of the southern courts.

There were no more powerful moments in the Birmingham episode than during the closing days of the campaign, when Negro youngsters ran after white policemen, asking to be locked up. There was an element of unmalicious mischief in this. The Negro youngsters, although perfectly willing to submit to imprisonment, knew that we had already filled up the jails, and that the police had no place left to take them.

When, for decades, you have been able to make a man compromise his manhood by threatening him with a cruel and unjust punishment, and when suddenly he turns upon you and says: 'Punish me. I do not deserve it. But because I do not deserve it, I will accept it so that the world will know that I am right and you are wrong,' you hardly know what to do. You feel defeated and secretly ashamed. You know that this man is as good a man as you are; that from some mysterious source he has found the courage and the conviction to meet physical force with soul force.

So it was that, to the Negro, going to jail was no longer a disgrace but a badge of honor. The Revolution of the Negro not only attacked the external cause of his misery, but revealed him to himself. He was *somebody*. He had a sense of *somebodiness*. He was *impatient* to be free.

In the past decade, still another technique had begun to replace the old methods for thwarting the Negroes' dreams and aspirations. This is the method known as 'tokenism.' The dictionary interprets the word 'token' in the following manner: 'A symbol. Indication, evidence, as a token of friendship, a keepsake. A piece of metal used in place of a coin, as for paying carfare on conveyances operated by those who sell the tokens. A sign, a mark, emblem, memorial, omen.'

When the Supreme Court modified its decision on school desegregation by approving the Pupil Placement Law, it permitted tokenism to corrupt its intent. It meant that Negroes could be handed the glitter of metal symbolizing the true coin, and authorizing a short-term trip toward democracy. But he who sells you the token instead of the coin always retains the power to revoke its worth, and to command you to get off the bus before you have reached your destination. Tokenism is a promise to pay. Democracy, in its finest sense, is payment.

The Negro wanted to feel pride in his race? With tokenism, the solution was simple. If all twenty million Negroes would keep looking at Ralph Bunche, the one man in so exalted a post would generate such a volume of pride that it could be cut into portions and served to everyone. A judge here and a judge there; an executive behind a polished desk in a carpeted office; a high government administrator with a toehold on a cabinet post; one student in a Mississippi university lofted there by an army; three Negro children admitted to the whole high-school system of a major city – all these were tokens used to obscure the persisting reality of segregation and discrimination.

For a decade the hard struggles had culminated in limited gains, which, if they advanced at all, crawled sluggishly forward. Schools, jobs, housing, voting rights and political positions – in each of these areas, manipulation with tokenism was the rule. Negroes had begun to feel that a policy was crystallizing, that all their struggles had brought them merely to a new level in which a selected few would become educated, honored and integrated to represent and substitute for the many.

Those who argue in favor of tokenism point out that we must begin somewhere; that it is unwise to spurn any breakthrough, no matter how limited. This position has a certain validity, and the Negro freedom movement has more often than not attained broad victories which had small beginnings. There is a critical distinction, however, between a modest start and tokenism. The tokenism Negroes condemn is recognizable because it is an end in itself. Its purpose is not to begin a process, but instead to end the process of protest and pressure. It is a hypocritical gesture, not a constructive first step.

I have gone into the Negro's resentment of tokenism at some length for I believe that analyzing his feelings about it will help to elucidate the uncompromising position he takes today. I think it will explain why he believes that half a loaf is no bread. I think it will justify his conviction that he must not turn back.

As I write, at the end of the first long season of Revolution, the Negro is not unmindful of or indifferent to the progress that has already been made. He notes with approval the radical change in the administration's approach to civil rights, and the small but visible gains being made on various fronts across the country. If he is still saying, 'Not enough,' it is because he does not feel that he should be expected to be *grateful* for the halting and inadequate attempts of his society to catch up with the basic rights he ought to have inherited automatically, centuries ago, by virtue of his membership in the human family and his American birthright.

In this conviction, he subscribes to the words of President Kennedy, uttered on June 11, 1963, only a few months before his tragic death: 'We are confronted primarily with a moral issue. It is as old as the Scriptures and is as clear as the American Constitution. The heart of the question is whether all Americans are to be afforded equal rights and equal opportunities . . . Those who do nothing are inviting shame as well as violence. Those who act boldly are recognizing right as well as reality.'

II

For a hundred years since emancipation, Negroes had searched for the elusive path to freedom. They knew that they had to fashion a body of tactics suitable for their unique and special conditions. The words of the Constitution had declared them free, but life had told them that they were a twice-burdened people – they lived in the lowest stratum of society, and within it they were additionally imprisoned by a caste of color.

For decades the long and winding trails led to dead ends. Booker T. Washington, in the dark days that followed Reconstruction, advised them: 'Let down your buckets where you are.' Be content, he said in effect, with doing well what the times permit you to do at all. However, this path, they soon felt, had too little freedom in its present and too little promise in its future.

Dr. W. E. B. Du Bois, in his earlier years at the turn of the century, urged the 'talented tenth' to rise and pull behind it the mass of the race. His doctrine served somewhat to counteract the apparent resignation of Booker T. Washington's philosophy. Yet, in the very nature of Du Bois's outlook there was no role for the whole people. It was a tactic for an aristocratic elite who would themselves be benefited while leaving behind the 'untalented' 90 percent.

After the First World War, Marcus Garvey made an appeal to the race that had the virtue of rejecting concepts of inferiority. He called for a return to Africa and a resurgence of race pride. His movement attained mass dimensions, and released a powerful emotional response because it touched a truth which had long been dormant in the mind of the Negro. There was reason to be proud of their heritage as well as of their bitterly won achievements in America. Yet his plan was doomed because an exodus to Africa in the twentieth century by a people who had struck roots for three and a half centuries in the New World did not have the ring of progress.

With the death of the Garvey movement, the way opened for the development of the doctrine which held the center of the stage for almost thirty years. This was the doctrine, consistently championed and ably conducted by the National Association for the Advancement of Colored People, that placed its reliance on the Constitution and the federal law. Under this doctrine, it was felt that the federal courts were the vehicle that could be utilized to combat oppression, particularly in southern states, which were operating under the guise of legalistics to keep the Negro down.

Under brilliant and dedicated leadership, the N.A.A.C.P. moved relentlessly to win many victories in the courts. The most notable of these established the right of the Negro to participate in national elections, striking down evasive devices such as the 'grandfather clause,' white primaries and others. Beyond doubt, the doctrine of change through legal recourse reached flood tide in the education decisions. Yet the failure of the nation, over a decade, to implement the majestic implications of these decisions caused the slow ebb of the Negro's faith in litigation as the dominant method to achieve his freedom. In his eyes, the doctrine of legal change had become the doctrine of slow token change and, as a sole weapon of struggle, now proved its unsuitability. At the time of this growing realization, during the mid-fifties, Negroes were in the grip of a crisis. Their movement no longer had a promising basic doctrine, a detailed and charted course pointing the way to their freedom.

It is an axiom of social change that no revolution can take place without a methodology suited to the circumstances of the period. During the fifties many voices offered substitutes for the tactic of legal recourse. Some called for a colossal blood bath to cleanse the nation's ills. To support their advocacy of violence and its incitement, they pointed to an historical tradition reaching back from the American Civil War to Spartacus in Rome. But the Negro in the South in 1955, assessing the power of the forces arrayed against him, could not perceive the slightest prospect of victory in this approach. He was unarmed, unorganized, untrained, disunited and, most important, psychologically and morally unprepared for the deliberate spilling of blood. Although his desperation had prepared him with the courage to die for freedom if necessary, he was not willing to commit himself to racial suicide with no prospect of victory.

Perhaps even more vital in the Negro's resistance to violence was the force of his deeply rooted spiritual beliefs. In Montgomery, after a courageous woman, Rosa Parks, had refused to move to the back of the bus, and so began the revolt that led to the boycott of 1955–56, the Negro's developing campaign against that city's racial injustice was based in the churches of the community. Throughout the South, for some years prior to Montgomery, the Negro church had emerged with increasing impact in the civil-rights struggle. Negro ministers, with a growing awareness that the true witness of a Christian life is the projection of a social gospel, had accepted leadership in the fight for racial justice, had played important roles in a number of N.A.A.C.P. groups, and were making their influence felt throughout the freedom movement.

The doctrine they preached was a nonviolent doctrine. It was not a doctrine that made their followers yearn for revenge but one that called upon them to champion change. It was not a doctrine that asked an eye for an eye but one that summoned men to seek to open the eyes of blind prejudice. The Negro turned his back on force not only because he knew he could not win his freedom through physical force but also because he believed that through physical force he could lose his soul.

There were echoes of Marcus Garvey in another solution proffered the Negro during this period of crisis and change. The Black Muslims, convinced that an interracial society promised nothing but tragedy and frustration for the Negro, began to urge a permanent separation of the races. Unlike Garvey's prescription, the Muslims appeared to believe the separation could be achieved in this country without a long sea voyage to Africa, but their message resembled Garvey's in another respect: It won only fractional support from the Negro community. Most of those to whom the Muslims appealed were in fact expressing resentment for the lack of militancy which had long prevailed in the freedom movement. When the Negroes' fighting spirit soared in the summer of 1963, the appeal of the Muslims declined precipitously. Today, as I travel throughout the country, I am struck by how few American Negroes (except in a handful of big-city ghettos) have even heard of the Muslim movement, much less given allegiance to its pessimistic doctrine.

Yet another tactic was offered the Negro. He was encouraged to seek unity with the millions of disadvantaged whites of the South, whose basic need for social change paralleled his own. Theoretically, this proposal held a measure of logic, for it is undeniable that great masses of southern whites exist in conditions scarcely better than those which afflict the Negro. But the rationale of this theory wilted under the heat of fact. The need for immediate change was more urgently felt and more bitterly realized by the Negro than by the exploited white. As individuals, the whites could better their situation without the barrier that society places in front of a man whose racial identification by color is inescapable. Moreover, the underprivileged southern whites saw the color that separated them from Negroes more clearly than they saw the circumstances that bound them together in mutual interest. Negroes were therefore forced to face the fact that, in the South, they must move without allies; and yet the coiled power of state force made such a prospect appear both futile and quixotic.

III

Fortunately, history does not pose problems without eventually producing solutions. The disenchanted, the disadvantaged and the disinherited seem, at times of deep crisis, to summon up some sort of genius that enables them to perceive and capture the appropriate weapons to carve out their destiny. Such was the peaceable weapon of nonviolent direct action, which materialized almost overnight to inspire the Negro, and was seized in his outstretched hands with a powerful grip.

Nonviolent action, the Negro saw, was the way to supplement – not replace – the process of change through legal recourse. It was the way to divest himself of passivity without arraying himself in vindictive force. Acting in concert with fellow Negroes to assert himself as a citizen, he would embark on a militant program to demand the rights which were his: in the streets, on the buses, in the stores, the parks and other public facilities.

The religious tradition of the Negro had shown him that the nonviolent resistance of the early Christians had constituted a moral offensive of such overriding power that it shook the Roman Empire. American history had taught him that nonviolence in the form of boycotts and protests had confounded the British monarchy and laid the basis for freeing the colonies from unjust domination. Within his own century, the nonviolent ethic of Mahatma Gandhi and his followers had muzzled the guns of the British Empire in India and freed more than three hundred and fifty million people from colonialism.

Like his predecessors, the Negro was willing to risk martyrdom in order to move and stir the social conscience of his community and the nation. Instead of submitting to surreptitious cruelty in thousands of dark jail cells and on countless shadowed street corners, he would force his oppressor to commit his brutality openly – in the light of day – with the rest of the world looking on.

Acceptance of nonviolent direct action was proof of a certain sophistication on the part of the Negro masses; for it showed that they dared to break with the old, ingrained concepts of our society. The eye-for-an-eye philosophy, the impulse to defend oneself when attacked, has always been held as the highest measure of American manhood. We are a nation that worships the frontier tradition, and our heroes are those who champion justice through violent retaliation against injustice. It is not simple to adopt the credo that moral force has as much strength and virtue as the capacity to return a physical blow; or that to refrain from hitting back requires more will and bravery than the automatic reflexes of defense.

Yet there is something in the American ethos that responds to the strength of moral force. I am reminded of the popular and widely respected novel and film *To Kill a Mockingbird*. Atticus Finch, a white southern lawyer, confronts a group of his neighbors who have become a lynch-crazed mob, seeking the life of his Negro client. Finch, armed with nothing more lethal than a lawbook, disperses the mob with the force of his moral courage, aided by his small daughter, who, innocently calling the would-be lynchers by name, reminds them that they are individual men, not a pack of beasts.

To the Negro in 1963, as to Atticus Finch, it had become obvious that nonviolence could symbolize the gold badge of heroism rather than the white feather of cowardice. In addition to being consistent with his religious precepts, it served his need to act on his own for his own liberation. It enabled him to transmute hatred into constructive energy, to seek not only to free himself but to free his oppressor from his sins. This transformation, in turn, had the marvelous effect of changing the face of the enemy. The enemy the Negro faced became not the individual who had oppressed him but the evil system which permitted that individual to do so.

The argument that nonviolence is a coward's refuge lost its force as its heroic and often perilous acts uttered their wordless but convincing rebuttal in Montgomery, in the sit-ins, on the freedom rides, and finally in Birmingham.

There is a powerful motivation when a suppressed people enlist in an army that marches under the banner of nonviolence. A nonviolent army has a magnificent universal quality. To join an army that trains its adherents in the methods of violence, you must be of a certain age. But in Birmingham, some of the most valued foot soldiers were youngsters ranging from elementary pupils to teenage high school and college students. For acceptance in the armies that maim and kill, one must be physically sound, possessed of straight limbs and accurate vision. But in Birmingham, the lame and the halt and the crippled could and did join up. Al Hibbler, the sightless singer, would never have been accepted in the United States Army or the army of any other nation, but he held a commanding position in our ranks.

In armies of violence, there is a caste of rank. In Birmingham, outside of the few generals and lieutenants who necessarily directed and coordinated operations, the regiments of the demonstrators marched in democratic phalanx. Doctors marched with window cleaners. Lawyers demonstrated with laundresses. Ph.D.'s and no-D.'s were treated with perfect equality by the registrars of the nonviolence movement.

As the broadcasting profession will confirm, no shows are so successful as those which allow for audience participation. In order to be somebody, people must feel themselves part of something. In the nonviolent army, there is room for everyone who wants to join up. There is no color distinction. There is no examination, no pledge, except that, as a soldier in the armies of violence is expected to inspect his carbine and keep it clean, nonviolent soldiers are called upon to examine and burnish their greatest weapons – their heart, their conscience, their courage and their sense of justice.

Nonviolent resistance paralyzed and confused the power structures against which it was directed. The brutality with which officials would have quelled the black individual became impotent when it could not be pursued with stealth and remain unobserved. It was caught – as a fugitive from a penitentiary is often caught – in gigantic circling spotlights. It was imprisoned in a luminous glare revealing the naked truth to the whole world. It is true that some demonstrators suffered violence, and that a few paid the extreme penalty of death. They were the martyrs of last summer who laid down their lives to put an end to the brutalizing of thousands who had been beaten and bruised and killed in dark streets and back rooms of sheriffs' offices, day in and day out, in hundreds of summers past.

The striking thing about the nonviolent crusade of 1963 was that so few felt the sting of bullets or the clubbing of billies and nightsticks. Looking back, it becomes obvious that the oppressors were restrained not only because the world was looking but also because, standing before them, were hundreds, sometimes thousands, of Negroes who for the first time dared to look back at a white man, eye to eye. Whether through a decision to exercise wise restraint or the operation of a guilty conscience, many a hand was stayed on a police club and many a fire hose was restrained from vomiting forth its pressure. That the Revolution was a comparatively bloodless one is explained by the fact that the Negro did not merely give lip service to nonviolence. The tactics the movement utilized, and that guided far-flung actions in cities dotted across the map, discouraged violence because one side would not resort to it and the other was so often immobilized by confusion, uncertainty and disunity.

Nonviolence had tremendous psychological importance to the Negro. He had to win and to vindicate his dignity in order to merit and enjoy his self-esteem. He had to let white men know that the picture of him as a clown – irresponsible, resigned and believing in his own inferiority – was a stereotype with no validity. This method was grasped by the Negro masses because it embodied the dignity of struggle, of moral conviction and self-sacrifice. The Negro was able to face his adversary, to concede to him a physical advantage and to defeat him because the superior force of the oppressor had become powerless.

To measure what this meant to the Negro may not

be easy. But I am convinced that the courage and discipline with which Negro thousands accepted nonviolence healed the internal wounds of Negro millions who did not themselves march in the streets or sit in the jails of the South. One need not participate directly in order to be involved. For Negroes all over this nation, to identify with the movement, to have pride in those who were the principals, and to give moral, financial or spiritual support were to restore to them some of the pride and honor which had been stripped from them over the centuries.

IV

In the light of last summer's successful crusade, one might ask why it took the Negro eight years to apply the lessons of the Montgomery boycott to the problems of Birmingham, and the nation's other Birminghams, north and south.

A methodology and philosophy of revolution is neither born nor accepted overnight. From the moment it emerges, it is subjected to rigorous tests, opposition, scorn and prejudice. The old guard in any society resents new methods, for old guards wear the decorations and medals won by waging battle in the accepted manner. Often opposition comes not only from the conservatives, who cling to tradition, but also from the extremist militants, who favor neither the old nor the new.

Many of these extremists misread the significance and intent of nonviolence because they failed to perceive that militancy is also the father of the nonviolent way. Angry exhortation from street corners and stirring calls for the Negro to arm and go forth to do battle stimulate loud applause. But when the applause dies, the stirred and the stirring return to their homes, and lie in their beds for still one more night with no progress in view. They cannot solve the problem they face because they have offered no challenge but only a call to arms, which they themselves are unwilling to lead, knowing that doom would be its reward. They cannot solve the problem because they seek to overcome a negative situation with negative means. They cannot solve the problem because they do not reach and move into sustained action the large groups of people necessary to attract attention and convey the determination of the majority. The conservatives who say, 'Let us not move so fast,' and the extremists who say, 'Let us go out and whip the world,' would tell you that they are as far apart as the poles. But there is a striking parallel: They accomplish nothing; for they do not reach the people who have a crying need to be free.

One factor that helps to explain why the Negro nationally did not embrace the nonviolent ethic, immediately after Montgomery, was a fallacious and dangerously divisive philosophy spread by those who were either dishonest or ignorant. This philosophy held that nonviolent, direct action was a *substitute* for all other approaches, attacking especially the legal methods that up to the mid-fifties had brought such important, decisive court rulings and laws into being. The best way to defeat an army is to divide it. Negroes as well as whites have compounded confusion and distorted reality by defending the legal approach and condemning direct action, or defending direct action and condemning the legal approach.

Direct action is not a substitute for work in the courts and the halls of government. Bringing about passage of a new and broad law by a city council, state legislature or the Congress, or pleading cases before the courts of the land, does not eliminate the necessity for bringing about the mass dramatization of injustice in front of a city hall. Indeed, direct action and legal action complement one another; when skillfully employed, each becomes more effective.

The chronology of the sit-ins confirms this observation. Spontaneously born, but guided by the theory of nonviolent resistance, the lunch-counter sit-ins accomplished integration in hundreds of communities at the swiftest rate of change in the civil-rights movement up to that time. Yet, many communities successfully resisted lunch-counter desegregation, and pressed charges against the demonstrators. It was correct and effective that demonstrators should fill the jails; but it was necessary that these foot soldiers for freedom not be deserted to languish there or to pay excessive penalties for their devotion. Indeed, by creative use of the law, it was possible to prove that officials combating the demonstrations were using the power of the police state to deny the Negro equal protection under the law. This brought many of the cases squarely under the jurisdiction of the Fourteenth Amendment. As a consequence of combining direct and legal action, far-reaching precedents were established, which served, in turn, to extend the areas of desegregation.

Another reason for the delay in applying the lessons of Montgomery was the feeling abroad in the land that the success of the bus boycott was an isolated phenomenon, and that the Negro elsewhere would never be willing to sacrifice in such extreme measure. When, in Albany, Georgia, in 1962, months of demonstrations and jailings failed to accomplish the goals of the movement, reports in the press and elsewhere pronounced nonviolent resistance a dead issue.

There were weaknesses in Albany, and a share of the responsibility belongs to each of us who participated. However, none of us was so immodest as to feel himself master of the new theory. Each of us expected that setbacks would be a part of the ongoing effort. There is no tactical theory so neat that a revolutionary struggle for a share of power can be won merely by pressing a row of buttons. Human beings with all their faults and strengths constitute the mechanism of a social movement. They must make mistakes and learn from them, make more mistakes and learn anew. They must taste defeat as well as success, and discover how to live with each. Time and action are the teachers.

When we planned our strategy for Birmingham months later, we spent many hours assessing Albany and trying to learn from its errors. Our appraisals not only helped to make our subsequent tactics more effective, but revealed that Albany was far from an unqualified failure. Though lunch counters remained segregated, thousands of Negroes were added to the voting-registration rolls. In the gubernatorial elections that followed our summer there, a moderate candidate confronted a rabid segregationist. By reason of the expanded Negro vote, the moderate defeated the segregationist in the city of Albany, which in turn contributed to his victory in the state. As a result, Georgia elected its first governor pledged to respect and enforce the law equally.

Our movement had been checked in Albany but not defeated. City authorities had been obliged to close down facilities such as parks, libraries and bus lines to avoid integration. The authorities were crippling themselves, denying facilities to the white population in order to obstruct our progress. Someone observed that Samuel Johnson had called parks 'the lungs of a city,' and that Albany would have to breathe again even though the air, too, be desegregated.

Even had nonviolent resistance been soundly defeated in Albany, the alacrity with which the bells were tolled for it must arouse suspicion. The prompt interment of the theory was not a judicious conclusion but an attack. Albany, in fact, had proved how extraordinary was the Negro response to the appeal of nonviolence. Approximately 5 percent of the total Negro population went willingly to jail. Were that percentage duplicated in New York City, some fifty thousand Negroes would overflow its prisons. If a people can produce from its ranks 5 percent who will go voluntarily to jail for a just cause, surely nothing can thwart its ultimate triumph.

If, however, the detractors of nonviolence fell into

error by magnifying temporary setbacks into cata-
strophic defeat, the adherents of the new theory must
avoid exaggerating its powers. When we speak of filling
the jails, we are talking of a tactic to be flexibly applied.
No responsible person would promise to fill all jails
everywhere at any time. Leaders indulge in bombast if
they do not take all circumstances into account before
calling upon their people to make a maximum sacrifice.
Filling jails means that thousands of people must leave
their jobs, perhaps to lose them, put off responsibilities,
undergo harrowing psychological experiences for which
law-abiding people are not routinely prepared. The mir-
acle of nonviolence lies in the degree to which people
will sacrifice under its inspiration, when the call is based
on judgment.

Negroes are human, not superhuman. Like all
people, they have differing personalities, diverse financial interests and varied aspirations. There are Negroes
who will never fight for freedom. There are Negroes
who will seek profit for themselves alone from the struggle. There are even some Negroes who will cooperate
with their oppressors. These facts should distress no one.
Every minority and every people has its share of oppor-
tunists, profiteers, freeloaders and escapists. The
hammer blows of discrimination, poverty and segregation must warp and corrupt some. No one can pretend
that because a people may be oppressed, every individual member is virtuous and worthy. The real issue is
whether in the great mass the dominant characteristics
are decency, honor and courage.

In 1963, once again life was proof that Negroes had their heroes, their masses of decent people, along with their lost souls. The doubts that millions had felt as to the efficacy of the nonviolent way were dissolved. And the Negro saw that by proving the sweeping and majestic power of nonviolence to bring about the beloved community, it might be possible for him to set an example to a whole world caught up in conflict.

V

In the entire country there was no place to compare with Birmingham. The largest industrial city in the South, Birmingham had become, in the thirties, a symbol for bloodshed when trade unions sought to organize. It was a community in which human rights had been trampled for so long that fear and oppression were as thick in its atmosphere as the smog from its factories. Its financial interests were interlocked with a power structure which spread throughout the South and radiated into the North.

The challenge to nonviolent, direct action could not have been staged in a more appropriate arena. In the summer of 1963, an army brandishing only the healing sword of nonviolence humbled the most powerful, the most experienced and the most implacable segregationists in the country. Birmingham was to emerge with a delicately poised peace, but without awaiting its implementation the Negro seized the weapon that had won that dangerous peace and swept across the land with it.

The victory of the theory of nonviolent direct action was a fact. Faith in this method had come to maturity in Birmingham. As a result, the whole spectrum of the civil-rights struggle would undergo basic change. Nonviolence had passed the test of its steel in the fires of turmoil. The united power of southern segregation was the hammer. Birmingham was the anvil.

The Days to Come

One hundred and fifty years ago, when the Negro was
a thing, a chattel whose body belonged to his white
master, there were certain slaveowners who worked out
arrangements whereby a slave could purchase himself,
and become a 'freedman.' An enterprising young man
who became enamored of a slave sweetheart worked
desperately – in what time he could find away from his
labors – and, over a period of years, amassed sufficient
capital to earn his own liberation and that of his be-
trothed. Many a Negro mother, after toiling from dawn
until sundown, would spend the remainder of the night
washing clothes and putting away the pennies and nick-
els so earned until, with the passage of years, a few
hundred dollars had been accumulated. Often she strug-
gled and sacrificed to purchase not her own freedom but
that of a son or daughter. The hard-earned dollars were
paid to the slaveowner in exchange for a legal instrument of manumission which declared its holder relieved
of the bondage of physical slavery.

As this movement grew, some Negroes devoted their
lives to the purchase and liberation of others. A servant
of Thomas Jefferson worked for some forty years and
earned ten thousand dollars, with which she was able

to obtain the liberation of nineteen fellow humans. Still later, a few dedicated and humanitarian white men took a crusade to the public for funds to ransom black people from the degradation which their abductors had imposed upon them. Even James Russell Lowell, who was opposed to compensated emancipation, wrote to a friend: 'If a man comes and asks us to help him buy his wife or his child, what are we to do?'

'Help me buy my mother,' or 'Help me buy my child,' was a poignant appeal. It brought the deep torture of black people's souls into stark and shocking focus for many whites to whom the horror of slavery had been emotionally remote.

As one approaches the emancipation of today's Negro from all those traumatic ties that still bind him to slaveries other than the physical, this shadowed footnote, this half-forgotten history of a system that bartered dignity for dollars, stands as a painful reminder of the capacity of society to remain complacent in the midst of injustice. Today's average American may well shudder to think that such tawdry transactions were acceptable to his grandparents' parents. Yet that same American may not realize that callous indifference to human suffering exists to this day, when people who consider themselves men of good will are still asking: 'What is the Negro willing to pay if we give him his freedom?'

This is not to say that today's society wants dollars and cents in order to grant the Negro his rights. But there is a terrible parallel between the outstretched and greedy hand of a slave trafficker who sold a Negro his own person, and the uplifted and admonishing finger of people who say today: 'What more will the Negro expect if he gains such rights as integrated schools, public facilities, voting rights and progress in housing? Will he, like Oliver Twist, demand more?'

What is implied here is the amazing assumption that society has the right to bargain with the Negro for the freedom which inherently belongs to him. Some of the most vocal liberals believe they have a valid basis for demanding that, in order to gain certain rights, the Negro ought to pay for them out of the funds of patience and passivity which he has stored up for so many years. What these people do not realize is that gradualism and moderation are not the answer to the great moral indictment which, in the Revolution of 1963, finally came to stand in the center of our national stage. What they do not realize is that it is no more possible to be half free than it is to be half alive.

In a sense, the well-meaning or the ill-meaning American who asks: 'What more will the Negro want?' or 'When will he be satisfied?' or 'What will it take to make these demonstrations cease?' is asking the Negro to purchase something that already belongs to him by every concept of law, justice and our Judaeo-Christian heritage. Moreover, he is asking the Negro to accept half the loaf and to pay for that half by waiting willingly for the other half to be distributed in crumbs over a hard and protracted winter of injustice. I would like to ask those people who seek to apportion to us the rights they have always enjoyed whether they believe that the framers of the Declaration of Independence intended that liberty should be divided into installments, doled out on a deferred-payment plan. Did not nature create birth as a single process? Is not freedom the negation of servitude? Does not one have to end totally for the other to begin?

It is because the Negro knows that no person – as well as no nation – can truly exist half slave and half free that he has embroidered upon his banners the significant word NOW. The Negro is saying that the time has come for our nation to take that firm stride into freedom – not simply toward freedom – which will pay a long-overdue debt to its citizens of color. Centuries ago, civilization acquired the certain knowledge that man had emerged from barbarity only to the degree that he recognized his relatedness to his fellow man. Civilization, particularly in the United States, has long possessed the material wealth and resources to feed, clothe and shelter all of its citizens. Civilization has endowed man with the capacity to organize change, to conceive and implement plans. It is ironic that, for so many years, the armed forces of this nation, even in time of war, were prisoners of the southern system of segregation. The military establishment could tear a man away from his wife and child, and reorient, within weeks, his entire mode of life and conduct. But not until World War II did the Army begin to conceive that it had the right, the obligation and the ability to say that a white man in uniform must respect the dignity of a black man in uniform.

We need a powerful sense of determination to banish

the ugly blemish of racism scarring the image of America. We can, of course, try to temporize, negotiate small, inadequate changes and prolong the time-table of freedom in the hope that the narcotics of delay will dull the pain of progress. We can try, but we shall certainly fail. The shape of the world will not permit us the luxury of gradualism and procrastination. Not only is it immoral, it will not work. It will not work because Negroes know they have the right to be free. It will not work because Negroes have discovered, in nonviolent direct action, an irresistible force to propel what has been for so long an immovable object. It will not work because it retards the progress not only of the Negro, but of the nation as a whole.

As certain as it is that a planned gradualism will not work, neither will unplanned spontaneity. When the locomotive of history roared through the nineteenth century and the first half of the twentieth, it left the nation's black masses standing forlornly at dismal terminals. They were unschooled, untrained, ill-housed, and ill-fed. The scientific achievements of today, particularly the explosive advance of automation, may be blessings to our economy, but for the Negro they are a curse. Years back, the Negro could boast that 350,000 of his race were employed by the railroads. Today, less than 50,000 work in this area of transportation. This is but a symbol of what has happened in the coal mines, the steel mills, the packing houses, in all industries that once employed large numbers of Negroes. The livelihood of millions has dwindled down to a frightening fraction because the unskilled and semiskilled jobs they filled have disappeared under the magic of automation. In that separate culture of poverty in which the half-educated Negro lives, an economic depression rages today. To deal with this disaster by opening some doors to all, and all doors to some, amounts merely to organizing chaos.

What is true in the field of employment also applies to housing. We cannot tap the ghettos in order to screen out a few representative individuals, leaving others to wait in grim shacks and tenements. Nor can the vast ghettos of many cities be turned inside out in one convulsive gesture, spilling people of all varieties into one torrent to flow wherever the social gravity pulls. Either of these courses – gradualism or directionless spontaneity – would generate social turmoil both for the deprived and for the privileged.

Solutions to the complex plight of the Negro will not be easy. This does not signify that they are impossible. Recognizing these complexities as challenges rather than as obstacles, we will make progress if we freely admit that we have no magic. We will make progress if we accept the fact that four hundred years of sinning cannot be canceled out in four minutes of atonement. Neither can we allow the guilty to tailor their atonement in such a manner as to visit another four seconds of deliberate hurt upon the victim.

II

Recently, Roy Wilkins and I appeared on the television program *Meet the Press*. There were the usual questions about how much more the Negro wants, but there seemed to be a new undercurrent of implications related to the sturdy new strength of our movement. Without the courtly complexities, we were, in effect, being asked if we could be trusted to hold back the surging tides of discontent so that those on the shore would not be made too uncomfortable by the buffeting and onrushing waves. Some of the questions implied that our leadership would be judged in accordance with our capacity to 'keep the Negro from going too far.' The quotes are mine, but I think the phrase mirrors the thinking of the panelists as well as of many other white Americans.

The show did not permit time for an adequate answer to the implications behind the question: 'What more does the Negro want?' When we say that the Negro wants absolute and immediate freedom and equality, not in Africa or in some imaginary state, but right here in this land today, the answer is disturbingly terse to people who are not certain they wish to believe it. Yet this is the fact. Negroes no longer are tolerant of or interested in compromise. American history is replete with compromise. As splendid as are the words of the Declaration of Independence, there are disquieting implications in the fact that the original phrasing was altered to delete a condemnation of the British monarch for his espousal of slavery. American history chronicles the Missouri Compromise, which permitted the spread of slavery to new states; the Hayes-Tilden Compromise, which withdrew the federal troops from the South and signaled the end of Reconstruction; the Supreme Court's compromise in *Plessy v. Ferguson*, which enunciated the infamous 'separate but equal' philosophy. These measures compromised not only the liberty of the Negro but the integrity of America. In the bursting mood that has overtaken the Negro in 1963, the word 'compromise' is profane and pernicious. The majority of Negro leadership is innately opposed to compromise. Even were this not true, no Negro leader today could divert the direction of the movement or its compelling and inspired forward motion.

Many of our white brothers misunderstand this fact because many of them fail to interpret correctly the nature of the Negro Revolution. Some believe that it is the work of skilled agitators who have the power to raise or lower the floodgates at will. Such a movement, maneuverable by a talented few, would not be a genuine revolution. This Revolution is genuine because it was born from the same womb that always gives birth to massive social upheavals – the womb of intolerable conditions and unendurable situations. In this time and circumstance, no leader or set of leaders could have acted as ringmasters, whipping a whole race out of purring contentment into leonine courage and action. If such credit is to be given to any single group, it might well go to the segregationists, who, with their callous and cynical code, helped to arouse and ignite the righteous wrath of the Negro. In this connection, I am reminded of something President Kennedy said to me at the White House following the signing of the Birmingham agreement.

'Our judgment of Bull Connor should not be too harsh,' he commented. 'After all, in his way, he has done a good deal for civil-rights legislation this year.'

It was the people who moved their leaders, not the leaders who moved the people. Of course, there were generals, as there must be in every army. But the command post was in the bursting hearts of millions of Negroes. When such a people begin to move, they create their own theories, shape their own destinies, and choose the leaders who share their own philosophy. A leader who understands this kind of mandate knows that he must be sensitive to the anger, the impatience, the frustration, the resolution that have been loosed in his people. Any leader who tries to bottle up these emotions is sure to be blown asunder in the ensuing explosion.

A number of commentators have implied that a band of militants has seized the offensive and that the 'sound and sensible' leaders are being drawn into action unwillingly in order to keep control from being wrested out of their hands. Certainly there are, and will continue to be, differences of opinion among Negro leaders, differences relating to certain specific, tactical moves; but to describe the meaning of recent events as the seizure of control by a few who have driven out the rest exaggerates the importance of the differences. The enemies of racial progress – and even some of its 'friends,' who are 'for it, but not so fast' – would delight in believing that there is chaos up front in the civil-rights ranks.

The hard truth is that the unity of the movement is

a remarkable feature of major importance. The fact that different organizations place varying degrees of emphasis on certain tactical approaches is not indicative of disunity. Unity has never meant uniformity. If it had, it would not have been possible for such dedicated democrats as Thomas Jefferson and George Washington, a radical such as Thomas Paine and an autocrat such as Alexander Hamilton to lead a unified American Revolution. Jefferson, Washington, Paine and Hamilton could collaborate because the urge of the colonials to be free had matured into a powerful mandate. This is what has happened to the determination of the Negro to liberate himself. When the cry for justice has hardened into a palpable force, it becomes irresistible. This is a truth which wise leadership and a sensible society ultimately come to realize.

In the current struggle, there is one positive course of action. There is no alternative, for the alternative would connote a rear march, and the Negro, far from being willing to retrogress, is not even willing to mark time. In this Revolution no plans have been written for retreat. Those who will not get into step will find that the parade has passed them by.

Someone once wrote: 'When you are right, you cannot be too radical; when you are wrong, you cannot be too conservative.' The Negro knows he is right. He has not organized for conquest or to gain spoils or to enslave those who have injured him. His goal is not to capture that which belongs to someone else. He merely wants and will have what is honorably his. When these long-withheld rights and privileges are looked upon as prizes he seeks from impertinent greed, only one answer can come from the depths of a Negro's being. That answer can be summarized in the hallowed American words: 'If this be treason, make the most of it.'

The sooner our society admits that the Negro Revolution is no momentary outburst soon to subside into placid passivity, the easier the future will be for us all.

III

Among the many vital jobs to be done, the nation must not only radically readjust its attitude toward the Negro in the compelling present, but must incorporate in its planning some compensatory consideration for the handicaps he has inherited from the past. It is impossible to create a formula for the future which does not take into account that our society has been doing something special *against* the Negro for hundreds of years. How then can he be absorbed into the mainstream of American life if we do not do something special *for* him now, in order to balance the equation and equip him to compete on a just and equal basis?

Whenever this issue of compensatory or preferential treatment for the Negro is raised, some of our friends recoil in horror. The Negro should be granted equality, they agree; but he should ask nothing more. On the surface, this appears reasonable, but it is not realistic. For it is obvious that if a man is entered at the starting line in a race three hundred years after another man, the first would have to perform some impossible feat in order to catch up with his fellow runner.

Several years ago, Prime Minister Nehru was telling me how his nation is handling the difficult problem of the untouchables, a problem not unrelated to the American Negro dilemma. The Prime Minister admitted that many Indians still harbor a prejudice against these long-oppressed people, but that it has become unpopular to exhibit this prejudice in any form. In part, this change in climate was created through the moral leadership of the late Mahatma Gandhi, who set an example for the nation by adopting an untouchable as his daughter. In part, it is the result of the Indian Constitution, which specifies that discrimination against the untouchables is a crime, punishable by imprisonment.

The Indian government spends millions of rupees annually developing housing and job opportunities in villages heavily inhabited by untouchables. Moreover, the Prime Minister said, if two applicants compete for entrance into a college or university, one of the applicants being an untouchable and the other of high caste, the school is required to accept the untouchable.

Professor Lawrence Reddick, who was with me during the interview, asked: 'But isn't that discrimination?'

'Well, it may be,' the Prime Minister answered. 'But this is our way of atoning for the centuries of injustices we have inflicted upon these people.'

America must seek its own ways of atoning for the injustices she has inflicted upon her Negro citizens. I do not suggest atonement for atonement's sake or because there is need for self-punishment. I suggest atonement as the moral and practical way to bring the Negro's standards up to a realistic level.

In facing the new American dilemma, the relevant question is not: 'What more does the Negro want?' but rather: 'How can we make freedom real and substantial for our colored citizens? What just course will ensure the greatest speed and completeness? And how do we combat opposition and overcome obstacles arising from the defaults of the past?'

New ways are needed to handle the issue because we have come to a new stage in the development of our nation and of one in ten of its people. The surging power of the Negro revolt and the genuineness of good will that has come from many white Americans indicate that the time is ripe for broader thinking and action.

The Negro today is not struggling for some abstract, vague rights, but for concrete and prompt improve-ment in his way of life. What will it profit him to be able to send his children to an integrated school if the family income is insufficient to buy them school clothes? What will he gain by being permitted to move to an integrated neighborhood if he cannot afford to do so because he is unemployed or has a low-paying job with no future? During the lunch-counter sit-ins in Greensboro, North Carolina, a nightclub comic observed that, had the demonstrators been served, some of them could not have paid for the meal. Of what advantage is it to the Negro to establish that he can be served in integrated restaurants, or accommodated in integrated hotels, if he is bound to the kind of financial servitude which will not allow him to take a vacation or even to take his wife out to dine? Negroes must not only have the right to go into any establishment open to the public, but they must also be absorbed into our economic system in such a manner that they can afford to exercise that right.

The struggle for rights is, at bottom, a struggle for opportunities. In asking for something special, the Negro is not seeking charity. He does not want to languish on welfare rolls any more than the next man. He does not want to be given a job he cannot handle. Neither, however, does he want to be told that there is no place where he can be trained to handle it. So with equal opportunity must come the practical, realistic aid which will equip him to seize it. Giving a pair of shoes to a man who has not learned to walk is a cruel jest.

Special measures for the deprived have always been accepted in principle by the United States. The National Urban League, in an excellent statement, has underlined the fact that we find nothing strange about the Marshall Plan and technical assistance to handicapped peoples around the world, and suggested that we can do no less for our own handicapped multitudes. Throughout history we have adhered to this principle. It was the principle behind land grants to farmers who fought in the Revolutionary Army. It was inherent in the establishment of child labor laws, social security, unemployment compensation, manpower retraining programs and countless other measures that the nation accepted as logical and moral.

During World War II, our fighting men were deprived of certain advantages and opportunities. To make up for this, they were given a package of veterans rights, significantly called a 'Bill of Rights.' The major features of this GI Bill of Rights included subsidies for trade school or college education, with living expenses provided during the period of study. Veterans were given special concessions enabling them to buy homes without cash, with lower interest rates and easier repayment terms. They could negotiate loans from banks to launch businesses, using the government as an endorser of any losses. They received special points to place them ahead in competition for civil-service jobs. They were provided with medical care and long-term financial grants if their physical condition had been impaired by their military service. In addition to these legally granted rights, a strong social climate for many years favored the preferential employment of veterans in all walks of life.

In this way, the nation was compensating the veteran for his time lost, in school or in his career or in business. Such compensatory treatment was approved by the majority of Americans. Certainly the Negro has been deprived. Few people consider the fact that, in addition to being enslaved for two centuries, the Negro was, during all those years, robbed of the wages of his toil. No amount of gold could provide an adequate compensation for the exploitation and humiliation of the Negro in America down through the centuries. Not all the wealth of this affluent society could meet the bill. Yet a price can be placed on unpaid wages. The ancient common law has always provided a remedy for the appropriation of the labor of one human being by another. This law should be made to apply for American Negroes. The payment should be in the form of a massive program by the government of special, compensatory measures which could be regarded as a settlement in accordance with the accepted practice of common law. Such measures would certainly be less expensive than any computation based on two centuries of unpaid wages and accumulated interest.

I am proposing, therefore, that, just as we granted a GI Bill of Rights to war veterans, America launch a broad-based and gigantic Bill of Rights for the Disadvantaged, our veterans of the long siege of denial.

Such a bill could adapt almost every concession given to the returning soldier without imposing an undue burden on our economy. A Bill of Rights for the Disadvantaged would immediately transform the conditions of Negro life. The most profound alteration would not reside so much in the specific grants as in the basic psychological and motivational transformation of the Negro. I would challenge skeptics to give such a bold new approach a test for the next decade. I contend that the decline in school dropouts, family breakups, crime rates, illegitimacy, swollen relief rolls and other social evils would stagger the imagination. Change in human psychology is normally a slow process, but it is safe to predict that, when a people is ready for change as the Negro has shown himself ready today, the response is bound to be rapid and constructive.

While Negroes form the vast majority of America's disadvantaged, there are millions of white poor who would also benefit from such a bill. The moral justification for special measures for Negroes is rooted in the robberies inherent in the institution of slavery. Many poor whites, however, were the derivative victims of slavery. As long as labor was cheapened by the involuntary servitude of the black man, the freedom of white labor, especially in the South, was little more than a myth. It was free only to bargain from the depressed base imposed by slavery upon the whole labor market. Nor did this derivative bondage end when formal slavery gave way to the de facto slavery of discrimination. To this day the white poor also suffer deprivation and the humiliation of poverty if not of color. They are chained by the weight of discrimination, though its badge of degradation does not mark them. It corrupts their lives, frustrates their opportunities and withers their education. In one sense it is more evil for them, because it has confused so many by prejudice that they have supported their own oppressors.

It is a simple matter of justice that America, in dealing creatively with the task of raising the Negro from backwardness, should also be rescuing a large stratum of the forgotten white poor. A Bill of Rights for the Disadvantaged could mark the rise of a new era, in which the full resources of the society would be used to attack the tenacious poverty which so paradoxically exists in the midst of plenty.

The nation will also have to find the answer to full employment, including a more imaginative approach than has yet been conceived for neutralizing the perils of automation. Today, as the unskilled and semiskilled Negro attempts to mount the ladder of economic security, he finds himself in competition with the white working man at the very time when automation is scrapping forty thousand jobs a week. Though this is perhaps the inevitable product of social and economic upheaval, it is an intolerable situation, and Negroes will not long permit themselves to be pitted against white workers for an ever-decreasing supply of jobs. The energetic and creative expansion of work opportunities, in both the public and private sectors of our economy, is an imperative worthy of the richest nation on earth, whose abundance is an embarrassment as long as millions of poor are imprisoned and constantly self-renewed within an expanding population.

In addition to such an economic program, a social-work apparatus on a large scale is required. Whole generations have been left behind as the majority of the population advanced. These lost generations have never learned basic social skills on a functional level – the skills of reading, writing, arithmetic; of applying for jobs; of exercising the rights of citizenship, including the right to vote. Moreover, rural and urban poverty has not only stultified lives; it has created emotional disturbances, many of which find expression in antisocial acts.

The most tragic victims are children, whose impoverished parents, frantically struggling day by day for food and a place to live, have been unable to create the stable home necessary for the wholesome growth of young minds.

Opportunities and the means to exploit them are, however, still inadequate to assure equality, justice and decency in our national life. There is an imperative need for legislation to outlaw our present grotesque legal mores. We find ourselves in a society where the supreme law of the land, the Constitution, is rendered inoperative in vast areas of the nation. State, municipal and county laws and practices negate constitutional mandates as blatantly as if each community were an independent medieval duchy. In the event that strong civil-rights legislation is written into the books in the session of Congress now sitting, and that a Bill of Rights for the Disadvantaged might follow, enforcement will still meet with massive resistance in many parts of the country.

In the thirties, the country was faced with a parallel challenge. Powerful and antagonistic elements all over the land were strongly resisting the efforts of workers to organize to secure a living wage and decent conditions of work. It is interesting to note that some of the states that today are opposing progress in civil rights were the same that defied the unions' efforts during the thirties. Then, as now, the task of penetrating thousands of communities in order to ensure the rights of their citizens over the opposition of hostile interests posed a substantial and complex challenge to federal power.

The national government found a method of solving this problem. The Wagner Act was written, establishing the rights of labor to organize. Regional labor boards were appointed, armed with the power to ascertain facts, conduct elections, issue binding orders and, through the utilization of these powers, to compel compliance. Of course, the strength of a newly aroused labor movement, with a well-sharpened strike weapon, stimulated cooperation. The twofold effect of a comprehensive law, backed by a zealous government and the power of organized labor, within a few short years transformed thousands of strife-torn, antilabor citadels into orderly, unionized communities.

A law designed to operate in the fashion of the Wagner Act may well be the answer to some of the problems of civil-rights enforcement during the next decade. Recently, Senator Harrison Williams of New Jersey presented a bill to the Senate incorporating many similar proposals. Other senators searching for legislative solutions should be encouraged to consider measures along these lines.

IV

The pattern of future action must be examined not only from the standpoint of the strengths inherent in the civil-rights movement, but simultaneously from a study of the resistance we have yet to face. While we can celebrate that the civil-rights movement has come of age, we must also recognize that the basic recalcitrance of the South has not yet been broken. True, substantial progress has been made: It is deeply significant that a powerful financial and industrial force has emerged in some southern regions, which is prepared to tolerate change in order to avoid costly chaos. This group in turn permits the surfacing of middle-class elements who are further splitting the monolithic front of segregation. Southern church, labor and human-relations groups today articulate sentiments that only yesterday would have been pronounced treasonable in the region. Nevertheless, a deeply entrenched social force, convinced that it need yield nothing of substantial importance, continues to dominate southern life. And even in the North, the will to preserve the status quo maintains a rocklike hardness underneath the cosmetic surface.

In order to assure that the work of democracy so well begun in the summer of 1963 will move forward steadily in the seasons to come, the Negro freedom movement will need to secure and extend its alliances with like-minded groups in the larger community. Already, in the complex dilemma of fast-paced progress and persistent poverty, the Negro has emerged as a dissatisfied, vibrant and powerful element, armed with a method for articulating and acting out his protest. His example has not gone unobserved by others, of all races, who live in equally desperate circumstances. Inevitably, before long, a broad-based legion of the deprived, white and

Negro, will coalesce and restructure an old order based too long on injustice.

In the case of organized labor, an alliance with the Negro civil-rights movement is not a matter of choice but a necessity. If Negroes have almost no rights in the South, labor has few more; if Negroes have inadequate political influence in Congress, labor is barely better off; if automation is a threat to Negroes, it is equally a menace to organized labor.

The withholding of support from the March on Washington by the National Council of the AFL-CIO was a blunder, and served to strengthen the prevalent feeling that organized labor, not only on the national level but frequently on the local level as well, is lacking today in statesmanship, vigor and modernity. This default is all the more noticeable because labor's history contains a rich record of understanding toward racial issues. When labor fought for recognition during the thirties and forties, and thus became the principal 'civil-rights' issue of the time, disadvantaged Negroes joined in its bitter struggles and shared every sacrifice. Negroes battling for their own recognition today have a right to expect more from their old allies. Nothing would hold back the forces of progress in American life more effectively than a schism between the Negro and organized labor.

Another necessary alliance is with the federal government. It is the obligation of government to move resolutely to the side of the freedom movement. There is a right and a wrong side in this conflict and the government does not belong in the middle.

Without the resources of the federal government, the task of achieving practical civil rights must overwhelm voluntary organization. It is not generally realized that the burden of court decision, such as the Supreme Court decision on school desegregation, places the responsibility on the individual Negro who is compelled to bring a suit in order to obtain his rights. In effect, the most impoverished Americans, facing powerfully equipped adversaries, are required to finance and conduct complex litigation that may involve tens of thousands of dollars. To have shaped remedies in this form for existing inequities in our national life was in itself a concession to segregationists. The unsound consequences of this procedure are hampering progress to this day. A solution can only be achieved if the government assumes the responsibility for all legal proceedings, facing the reality that the poor and the unemployed already fight an unequal daily struggle to stay alive. To be forced to accumulate resources for legal actions imposes intolerable hardships on the already overburdened.

Perhaps the most determining factor in the role of the federal government is the tone set by the chief executive in his words and his actions. In the past few years, I have met and talked with three presidents, and have grown increasingly aware of the play of their temperaments on their approach to civil rights, a cause that all three have espoused in principle.

No one could discuss racial justice with President Eisenhower without coming away with mixed emotions. His personal sincerity on the issue was pronounced, and he had a magnificent capacity to communicate it to individuals. However, he had no ability to translate it to the public, or to define the problem as a supreme domestic issue. I have always felt that he failed because he knew that his colleagues and advisers did not share his views, and he had no disposition to fight even for cherished beliefs. Moreover, President Eisenhower could not be committed to anything which involved a structural change in the architecture of American society. His conservatism was fixed and rigid, and any evil defacing the nation had to be extracted bit by bit with a tweezer because the surgeon's knife was an instrument too radical to touch this best of all possible societies.

President Kennedy was a strongly contrasted personality. There were, in fact, two John Kennedys. One presided in the first two years under pressure of the uncertainty caused by his razor-thin margin of victory. He vacillated, trying to sense the direction his leadership could travel while retaining and building support for his administration. However, in 1963, a new Kennedy had emerged. He had found that public opinion was not in a rigid mold. American political thought was not committed to conservatism, nor radicalism, nor moderation. It was above all fluid. As such it contained trends rather than hard lines, and affirmative leadership could guide it into constructive channels.

President Kennedy was not given to sentimental expressions of feeling. He had, however, a deep grasp of the dynamics of and the necessity for social change. His work for international amity was a bold effort on a world scale. His last speech on race relations was the most earnest, human and profound appeal for understanding and justice that any president has uttered since the first days of the Republic. Uniting his flair for leadership with a program of social progress, he was at his death undergoing a transformation from a hesitant leader with unsure goals to a strong figure with deeply appealing objectives.

The assassination of President Kennedy killed not only a man but a complex of illusions. It demolished the myth that hate and violence can be confined in an airtight chamber to be employed against but a few. Suddenly the truth was revealed that hate is a contagion; that it grows and spreads as a disease; that no society is so healthy that it can automatically maintain its immunity. If a smallpox epidemic had been raging in the South, President Kennedy would have been urged to avoid the area. There was a plague afflicting the South, but its perils were not perceived.

Negroes tragically know political assassination well. In the life of Negro civil-rights leaders, the whine of the bullet from ambush, the roar of the bomb have all too often broken the night's silence. They have replaced lynching as a political weapon. More than a decade ago, sudden death came to Mr and Mrs Harry T. Moore, N.A.A.C.P. leaders in Florida. The Reverend George Lee of Belzoni, Mississippi, was shot to death on the steps of a rural courthouse. The bombings multiplied. Nineteen sixty-three was a year of assassinations. Medgar Evers in Jackson, Mississippi; William Moore in Alabama; six Negro children in Birmingham – and who could doubt that these too were political assassinations?

The unforgivable default of our society has been its failure to apprehend the assassins. It is a harsh judgment, but undeniably true, that the cause of the indifference was the identity of the victims. Nearly all were Negroes. And so the plague spread until it claimed the most eminent American, a warmly loved and respected president. The words of Jesus 'Inasmuch as ye have done it unto one of the least of these my brethren, ye have done it unto me' were more than a figurative expression; they were a literal prophecy.

We were all involved in the death of John Kennedy. We tolerated hate; we tolerated the sick stimulation of violence in all walks of life; and we tolerated the differential application of law, which said that a man's life was sacred only if we agreed with his views. This may explain the cascading grief that flooded the country in late November. We mourned a man who had become the pride of the nation, but we grieved as well for ourselves because we knew we were sick.

In sadness and remorse the American people have searched for a monument big enough to honor John Kennedy. Airports, bridges, space centers and highways now bear his name. Yet the foundations for the most majestic tribute of all were laid in the days immediately following his death. Louis Harris, polling a cross section of the country for its reaction to the assassination, wrote that 'the death of President Kennedy produced a profound change in the thinking of the American people; a massive rejection of extremism from either right or left, accompanied by an individual sense of guilt for not working more for tolerance toward others.' If the tragically premature end of John Kennedy will prove to have so enlarged the sense of humanity of a whole people, that in itself will be a monument of enduring strength.

I had been fortunate enough to meet Lyndon Johnson during his tenure as vice president. He was not then a presidential aspirant, and was searching for his role under a man who not only had a four-year term to complete but was confidently expected to serve out yet another term as chief executive. Therefore, the essential issues were easier to reach, and were unclouded by political considerations.

His approach to the problem of civil rights was not identical with mine – nor had I expected it to be. Yet his careful practicality was nonetheless clearly no mask to conceal indifference. His emotional and intellectual involvement were genuine and devoid of adornment. It was conspicuous that he was searching for a solution to a problem he knew to be a major shortcoming in American life. I came away strengthened in my conviction that an undifferentiated approach to white southerners could be a grave error, all too easy for Negro leaders in the heat of bitterness. Later, it was Vice President Johnson I had in mind when I wrote in *The Nation* that the white South was splitting, and that progress could be furthered by driving a wedge between the rigid segregationists and the new white elements whose love of their land was stronger than the grip of old habits and customs.

Today, the dimensions of Johnson's leadership have spread from a region to a nation. His recent expressions, public and private, indicate that he has a comprehensive grasp of contemporary problems. He has seen that poverty and unemployment are grave and growing catastrophes, and he is aware that those caught most fiercely in the grip of this economic holocaust are Negroes. Therefore, he has set the twin goal of a battle against discrimination within the war against poverty.

I have no doubt that we may continue to differ concerning the tempo and the tactical design required to combat the impending crisis. But I do not doubt that the president is approaching the solution with sincerity, with realism and, thus far, with wisdom. I hope his course will be straight and true. I will do everything in my power to make it so by outspoken agreement whenever proper, and determined opposition whenever necessary.

v

For many months during the election campaign of 1960, my close friends urged me to declare my support for John Kennedy. I spent many troubled hours searching for the responsible and fair decision. I was impressed by his qualities, by many elements of his record, and by his program. I had learned to enjoy and respect his charm and his incisive mind. Beyond that I was personally obligated to him and to his brother, Robert Kennedy, for their intervention during my 1960 imprisonment in Georgia.

However, I felt that the weight of history was against a formal endorsement. No president except perhaps Lincoln had ever sufficiently given that degree of support to our struggle for freedom to justify our confidence. I had to conclude that the then known facts about Kennedy were not adequate to make an unqualified judgment in his favor. Today, I still deeply believe that the civil-rights movement must retain its independence. And yet, had President Kennedy lived, I would probably have endorsed him in the forthcoming election.

I did not arrive at this conclusion only because I learned to repose more confidence in President Kennedy. Perhaps more basic is the fact that a new stage in civil rights has been reached, which calls for a new policy. What has changed is our strength. The upsurge of power in the civil-rights movement has given it greater maneuverability, and substantial security. It is now strong enough to form alliances, to make commitments in exchange for pledges, and if the pledges are unredeemed, it remains powerful enough to walk out without being shattered or weakened.

Negroes have traditionally positioned themselves too far from the inner arena of political decision. Few other minority groups have maintained a political aloofness and a nonpartisan posture as rigidly and as long as Negroes. The Germans, Irish, Italians, and Jews, after a period of acclimatization, moved inside political formations and exercised influence. Negroes, partly by choice but substantially by exclusion, have operated outside of the political structures, functioning instead essentially as a pressure group with limited effect.

For some time, this reticence protected the Negro from corruption and manipulation by political bosses. The cynical district leader directing his ignorant flock to vote blindly at his dictation is a relatively rare phenomenon in Negro life. The very few Negro political bosses have no gullible following. Those who give them support do so because they are persuaded that these men are their only available forthright spokesmen. By and large, Negroes remain essentially skeptical, issue-oriented, and independent-minded. Their lack of formal learning is no barrier when it comes to making intelligent choices among alternatives.

The Negroes' real problem has been that they have seldom had adequate choices. Political life, as a rule, did not attract the best elements of the Negro community, and white candidates who represented their views were few and far between. However, in avoiding the trap of domination by unworthy leaders, Negroes fell into the bog of political inactivity. They avoided victimization by any political group by withholding a significant commitment to any organization or individual.

The price they paid was reflected in the meager influence they could exercise for a positive program. But in the more recent years, as a result of their direct-action programs, their political potentiality has become manifest both to themselves and to the political leadership.

An active rethinking is taking place in all Negro circles concerning their role in political life. The conclusion is already certain: It is time for Negroes to abandon abstract political neutrality and become less timid about voting alliances. If we bear in mind that alliance does not mean reliance, our independence will remain inviolate. We can and should selectively back candidates whose record justifies confidence. We can, because of our strength; we should, because those who work with us must feel we can help them concretely. Conversely, those who deny us their support should not feel that no one will get our help, but instead they must understand that when they spurn us it is likely not only that they will lose, but that their opponent will gain.

The Negro potential for political power is now substantial. Negroes are strategically situated in large cities, especially in the North but also in the South, and these cities in turn are decisive in state elections. These same states are the key in a presidential race, and frequently determine the nomination. This unique factor gives Negroes enormous leverage in the balance of power. The effects of this leverage are already evident. In South Carolina, for example, the 10,000-vote margin that gave President Kennedy his victory in 1960 was the Negro vote. Since then, some half a million new Negro voters have been added to southern registration rolls. Today, a shift in the Negro vote could upset the outcome of several state contests, and affect the result of a presidential election.

Moreover, the subjective elements of political power – persistence, aggressiveness and discipline – are also attributes of the new movement. Political leaders are infinitely respectful toward any group that has an abundance of energy to ring doorbells, man the street corners and escort voters to the polls. Negroes in their demonstrations and voter-registration campaigns have been acquiring excellent training in just these tasks. They also have discipline perhaps beyond that of any other group, because it has become a condition of survival. Consider the political power that would be generated if the million Americans who marched in 1963 also put their energy directly into the electoral process.

Already, in some states and cities in the South, a de facto alliance of Negro and sympathetic white voters has elected a new type of local official – nonintegrationist, but nonsegregationist too. As Negroes extend their energetic voting and registration campaigns, and attain bloc-voting importance, such officials will move from dead center and slowly find the courage to stand unequivocally for integration.

On the national scene, the Congress today is dominated by southern reactionaries whose control of the key committees enables them to determine legislation. Disenfranchisement of the Negro and the nonexercise of the vote by poor whites have permitted the southern congressman to wrest his election from a tiny group, which he manipulates easily to return him again and again to office. United with northern reactionaries, these unrepresentative legislators have crippled the country by blocking urgently needed action. Only with the growth of an enlightened electorate, white and

Negro together, can we put a quick end to this century-old stranglehold of a minority on the nation's legislative processes.

There are those who shudder at the idea of a political bloc, particularly a Negro bloc, which conjures up visions of racial exclusiveness. This concern is, however, unfounded. Not exclusiveness but effectiveness is the aim of bloc voting; by forming a bloc a minority makes its voice heard. The Negro minority will unite for political action for the same reason that it will seek to function in alliance with other groups – because in this way it can compel the majority to listen.

It is well to remember that blocs are not unique in American life, nor are they inherently evil. Their purposes determine their moral quality. In past years, labor, farmers, businessmen, veterans, and various national minorities have voted as blocs on various issues, and many still do. If the objectives are good, and each issue is decided on its own merits, a bloc is a wholesome force on the political scene. Negroes are, in fact, already voting spontaneously as a bloc. They voted overwhelmingly for President Kennedy, and before that for President Roosevelt. Development as a conscious bloc would give them more flexibility, more bargaining power, more clarity and more responsibility in assessing candidates and programs. Moreover a deeper involvement as a group in political life will bring them more independence. Consciously and creatively developed, political power may well, in the days to come, be the most effective new tool of the Negro's liberation.

Because Negroes can quite readily become a compact, conscious and vigorous force in politics, they can do more than achieve their own racial goals. American politics needs nothing so much as an injection of the idealism, self-sacrifice and sense of public service which is the hall-mark of our movement. Until now, comparatively few major Negro leaders of talent and unimpeachable character have involved themselves actively in partisan politics. Such men as Judge William Hastie, Ralph Bunche, Benjamin Mays, A. Philip Randolph, to name but a few, have remained aloof from the political scene. In the coming period, they and many others must move out into political life as candidates and infuse it with their humanity, their honesty and their vision.

For whatever demands the Negro justly makes on his fellow citizens are not an effort to lift responsibility from himself. His tasks are still fundamental, involving risks and sacrifices which he has already proved himself prepared to make. In addition, he will have to learn new skills, new duties, and creatively and constructively to embrace a new way of life. Ask a prisoner released after years of confinement in jail what efforts he faces in taking on the privileges and responsibilities of freedom, and the enormity of the Negroes' task in the years ahead becomes clear.

VI

One aspect of the civil-rights struggle that receives little attention is the contribution it makes to the whole society. The Negro in winning rights for himself produces substantial benefits for the nation. Just as a doctor will occasionally reopen a wound, because a dangerous infection hovers beneath the half-healed surface, the revolution for human rights is opening up unhealthy areas in American life and permitting a new and wholesome healing to take place. Eventually the civil-rights movement will have contributed infinitely more to the nation than the eradication of racial injustice. It will have enlarged the concept of brotherhood to a vision of total interrelatedness. On that day, Canon John Donne's doctrine, 'no man is an islande,' will find its truest application in the United States.

In measuring the full implications of the civil-rights revolution, the greatest contribution may be in the area of world peace. The concept of nonviolence has spread on a mass scale in the United States as an instrument of change in the field of race relations. To date, only a relatively few practitioners of nonviolent direct action have been committed to its philosophy. The great mass have used it pragmatically as a tactical weapon, without being ready to live it.

More and more people, however, have begun to conceive of this powerful ethic as a necessary way of life in a world where the wildly accelerated development of nuclear power has brought into being weapons that can annihilate all humanity. Political agreements are no longer secure enough to safeguard life against a peril of such devastating finality. There must also be a philosophy, acceptable to the people, and stronger than resignation toward sudden death.

It is no longer merely the idealist or the doom-ridden who seeks for some controlling force capable of challenging the instrumentalities of destruction. Many are searching. Sooner or later all the peoples of the world, without regard to the political systems under which they live, will have to discover a way to live together in peace.

Man was born into barbarism when killing his fellow man was a normal condition of existence. He became endowed with a conscience. And he has now reached the day when violence toward another human being must become as abhorrent as eating another's flesh.

Nonviolence, the answer to the Negroes' need, may become the answer to the most desperate need of all humanity.